INTERNAL CONSULTING FOR HRD PROFESSIONALS

Tools, Techniques, and Strategies for Improving Organizational Performance

INTERNAL CONSULTING FOR HRD PROFESSIONALS

Tools, Techniques, and Strategies for Improving Organizational Performance

Jerry W. Gilley, Ed.D.
President
Trilogy Consulting Group

Amy J. Coffern, M.A.
Principal
William M. Mercer, Incorporated

ASTD

AMERICAN SOCIETY
FOR TRAINING AND
DEVELOPMENT

IRWIN
Professional Publishing
Burr Ridge, Illinois
New York, New York

Sponsoring editor: Cynthia A. Zigmund
Project editor: Karen J. Nelson
Production manager: Jon Christopher
Designer: Jeanne M. Rivera
Art manager: Kim Meriwether
Art studio: Graphics Plus
Compositor: Precision Typographers
Typeface: 11/13 Palatino
Printer: Arcata Graphics/Kingsport

Library of Congress Cataloging-in-Publication Data

Gilley, Jerry W.
　　Internal consulting for HRD professionals : tools, techniques, and strategies for improving organizational performance / Jerry W. Gilley and Amy J. Coffern.
　　　　p.　　cm.
　　Includes bibliographical references and index.
　　ISBN 1-55623-758-8
　　1. Business consultants.　2. Personnel management.　I. Coffern, Amy J.　II. Title.
HD69.C6G54　1994
658.3—dc20

93-5595

Printed in the United States of America
　　3　4　5　6　7　8　9　0　AGK　0　9　8　7　6　5

Preface

This book is designed to help human resource development (HRD) practitioners make a transition to "internal consultants." This transition is important because it is internal consultants who can influence an organization's decision-makers and impact the bottom line by changing behaviors—by "making a difference."

To learn these skills, you must:

- Understand the evolution of HRD within an organization.
- Identify how an internal consultant participates in the four processes of HRD.
- Learn how to build positive client relationships.
- Use strategic planning, project management, and marketing as tools of change.
- Develop good problem-solving skills.

The role of internal consultant is a serious and complex one, consisting of eight sub-roles: (1) analyst, (2) designer, (3) implementer, (4) transfer agent, (5) marketer, (6) strategic planner, (7) project manager, and (8) process consultant. To effectively perform as an internal consultant, you must become aware of and competent in each of these eight sub-roles. This book is designed to help you do that.

We describe these sub-roles and the skills named above to help you become an internal consultant in your organization. In addition, we look at ideas and steps that internal consultants can follow to better use the four processes of HRD and to integrate three tools available to internal consultants (strategic planning, marketing, and project management), and show the importance of building and keeping good client relationships.

Chapter 1 is an overview of the book. In Chapter 2, we discuss the eight purposes of an internal consultant. We also discuss the types of organizations where internal consultants exist and take an in-depth look at the evolution of HRD and internal consultants.

The second part of the book focuses on the four processes of HRD (analysis, design, implementation, and evaluation—transfer of learning) and the internal consultant's role in these processes. We discuss each of these processes and show how internal consultants can use each one to improve employee performance and enhance organizational effectiveness.

We also discuss transfer of learning and how it impacts organizational effectiveness and individual productivity. Part of this discussion includes why transfer of learning is a problem and how evaluation can be used to improve the transfer of learning. We also discuss the barriers to learning transfer and supply recommendations for overcoming the barriers before, during, and after training programs and other interventions. Finally, we discuss why it is important to prepare employees for change and how to improve the training process and transfer of learning on the job.

Part three of the book reviews three tools of HRD: strategic planning, project management, and marketing. Each of these tools can help you improve performance and enhance organizational effectiveness. These tools are designed to improve your image and credibility as an internal consultant, improve your strategic focus, and help you better plan, manage, and implement projects.

We conclude the book with a discussion of how to set up and manage client relationships. This discussion is an in-depth look at the interpersonal skills required to be successful. These chapters will help you understand the problem-solving process and how your interpersonal and consulting skills can help provide solutions to problems facing the organization. Finally, we discuss the values you must maintain to be successful.

ACKNOWLEDGMENTS

We would like to thank Robert Brinkerhoff, Professor, Western Michigan University, for his insight and inspiration about this topic. Without his continuous support, this project would never have been completed. We would also like to thank our professional staff, Kathy Mann, Donna Kosick, and Leilani Costello, Debbie Stone, the supervisor of word processing at William M. Mercer,

Incorporated, in Chicago, along with Eskin Smyles, Helene Trottier, Linda Whitlow, Yolanda Witherspoon, and Susan Blake, for their efforts in producing this document. Finally, we would like to acknowledge Ron Walker, executive vice president, William M. Mercer, Incorporated, for his encouragement and continuous support throughout this project.

Contents

The Role of the Internal Consultant in Today's Organization

The field of human resource development (HRD) has evolved to become a critical part of the success equation in many organizations. As a result, HRD is viewed by senior management as an important strategic approach to improving productivity and quality, causing many organizations to see the HRD professional in a more positive light. Gone are the days of stand-up trainers with limited professional experience and a lack of organizational sophistication. In their place are professional HRD practitioners.

One role, which is increasing in importance and value, is that of the internal consultant. But as internal consultants, HRD practitioners are often surprised to find themselves in a very different world, which complicates the transition to this new role. Now, they must search for problems and synthesize solutions to them. Instead of knowing all the answers to the right questions, they must find answers to questions that cannot be addressed by their classroom experience. Instead of being in control, they are of service to the organization; they must now focus on the organization's desired changes rather than on individual improvement.

Internal consultants are on unfamiliar turf. No longer in their familiar, comfortable classroom, they may feel overwhelmed, inundated by the complexities of the problems they must solve. There may be a tendency to retreat to the classroom (avoidance) or bring an easy classroom solution to difficult problems (simplification).

Either as learning specialists or instructional designers, they had time to plan, design, evaluate, and adjust. As internal consultants, however, they are often asked to make decisions in seconds. People may not respond or behave exactly the way the textbook model predicts.

PURPOSE OF THE INTERNAL CONSULTANT

One of the most critical questions that internal consultants must address is, "Why am I here?" Answering this question will give you a better understanding of your purpose in the organization. As you look at this question, you will be better able to articulate the various tasks and functions you are required to perform. You can then rank them in order of their importance and make critical decisions about how to spend your time.

In Chapter 2, we discuss the eight purposes of the internal consultant. These purposes are arranged in a hierarchy according to the influence each has on organizational change. We discuss why each of these purposes is important to carrying out your professional goals. We then look at the types of organizations where internal consulting might be present and discuss how management sees its employees and the relationship of its employees to the organization. We discuss the implications of each type of organization on the role of the internal consultant.

Finally in Chapter 2, we take an in-depth look at the evolution of HRD. We supply evidence of where the internal consultant role emerges in this evolution. This will help you to decide whether or not the internal consulting role is a viable one in your organization. In other words, the type of organization you're in and the evolution of HRD within your organization are critical components when deciding whether or not the internal consulting role is one you should seriously consider taking part in or developing.

FOUR PROCESSES OF HRD

Much has been written about the field of HRD. Some important competency studies and extensive research have been conducted on this emerging field. One thing that seems to be consistent in this research is that HRD consists of four primary processes: (1) analysis, (2) design, (3) implementation, and (4) evaluation. In Chapters 3, 4, and 5, we discuss each of these processes.

Analysis Process

In Chapter 3, we discuss how internal consultants can use the analysis process to improve organizational effectiveness. To do this, we believe internal consultants must first begin to think analytically. You must ask yourself:

1. What is a problem?
2. Where is the pain?
3. What evidence do you have to support your point of view or perceptions?
4. What does the organizational leadership prefer?
5. How should you best proceed?

As this discussion unfolds, we focus our attention on tools and techniques you can use during the analysis process and the types of analyses most often conducted by internal consultants. We also address the three types of gaps that most commonly exist in today's organizations: (1) performance, (2) management, and (3) organizational.

Design and Implementation Process

In Chapter 4, we discuss the design and implementation processes of HRD, focusing on how internal consultants can use the design and implementation processes to improve individual performance, productivity, and organizational effectiveness. We also provide information about how internal consultants can use employee experience as a change strategy and about the types of activities most often used during these processes. Finally, we show how the internal consultant's role evolves from designer and implementor to performance manager. We discuss the importance of performance feedback, *antecedents*, positive reinforcement, and consequences in improving employee performance.

Evaluation to Transfer of Learning Process

In Chapter 5, we depart from looking at how evaluation can be used by internal consultants and turn to an in-depth discussion of the transfer of learning and how it impacts organizational effectiveness and individual productivity. We begin our discussion by examining why transfer of learning is a problem. We demonstrate how evaluation can be used as a tool for improving the transfer of learning. We embrace the evaluation phase of HRD, but not in the traditional manner.

Also in this chapter, we look at the barriers to learning transfer and why these barriers prevent employees from integrating and applying new skills and knowledge. Next, we examine a model for change that explains the internal consultant's role in learning transfer. We supply recommendations for creating change before, during, and after training programs and other interventions. We discuss why it's important to prepare employees for a change and how to improve the training process by providing strategies for improving learning transfer on the job. Finally, we conclude this chapter by challenging you to focus your attention on the problem of learning transfer.

THE THREE TOOLS OF HRD

As internal consultants, you have three critical tools that will help you improve organizational effectiveness: strategic planning, marketing, and project management. Each of these tools is designed to improve your strategic focus, improve your image and credibility as an internal consultant, and help you better plan, manage, and carry out projects.

Strategic Planning

In Chapter 6, we discuss the seven steps of strategic planning and why strategic planning is important for internal consultants. The seven steps are: (1) identify organizational values, (2) create an operational mission statement, (3) conduct environmental analyses, (4) identify goals and objectives, (5) identify action steps designed to accomplish the plan, (6) conduct reality checks of the plan, and (7) obtain feedback.

Strategic planning is a macro activity designed to align the internal consulting process with organizational strategic goals and objectives. By comparison, the marketing planning process discussed in Chapter 7 is a micro activity designed to improve the image and credibility of internal consultants. We believe both processes are critically important.

The Marketing Process

In Chapter 7, we apply the strategic marketing planning process to enhance the image and credibility of internal consultants. This activity means being client-focused and client-centered. We also discuss the importance of communication between internal consultants and their clients. These two activities serve as a foundation for the strategic marketing planning process.

We continue the chapter by taking a comprehensive look at how strategic marketing planning can be used as a process for change. We look at the importance of identifying your marketing mission. We also discuss how to conduct an operational audit of your organization, both internally and externally, to find the strengths and weaknesses of your HRD program as well as the opportunities and constraints that will enhance or restrict you.

Next, we discuss why it's important to identify marketing goals for internal consultants and critical marketing segments that can be impacted and influenced. This activity includes ranking various market segments when you have limited resources.

We also look at the four strategies that will improve the focus of internal consulting, including program, promotion, time and location, and price strategy. Each of these strategies combines to make up what we refer to as the *marketing mix*. We conclude Chapter 7 with a discussion of the critical decisions you must make to improve your image and credibility in the organization.

Project Management

The last tool we address is project management. In Chapter 8 we ask, "What is a project, and what is project management?" We also discuss the role of a project manager, because internal consultants are always engaged in planning, organizing, directing, coordinating, and implementing projects.

We discuss the four components of project management, which include planning, organizing, directing, and controlling, and why these are important to internal consultants. The majority of this chapter focuses on the tools, techniques, and processes used in project management, including (1) goal analysis, (2) stakeholder analysis, (3) risk analysis, and (4) project networking.

We discuss task identification and dependency relationships in and among tasks, followed by scheduling techniques such as front-loaded, rear-loaded, and level-loaded schedules. Finally, we conclude this chapter with the importance of developing correct project budgets and control procedures.

PROCESS CONSULTING IN HRD

In chapters 9 and 10, we introduce you to the "process consulting" activities of internal consultants: building and maintaining good client relationships and solving problems.

Building and Maintaining Client Relationships

Chapter 9 focuses on how process consulting can be used to manage the client relationship. We examine the skills needed to properly develop client relationships and how you can use those skills to set up rapport and trust with your clients. These skills include interpersonal skills (listening, questioning, communication, feedback, and negotiation) and presentation skills. Finally, we talk about how to *keep* clients happy. Your client's happiness is extremely critical to your success as an internal consultant.

Problem-Solving Process

In Chapter 10, we discuss how internal consultants can use the problem-solving process to improve performance, quality and to manage change. Managing change is perhaps one of the most critical and serious activities you will perform. It is important that you understand your role and responsibility in managing change within an organization.

We outline a six-step process that you can use to bring about change. The first step is to identify your client's situation. This is important in establishing the context, circumstances, and situation of your clients. Second, you must determine the desired objectives as a result of change, followed by showing solutions to your clients' problems. Fourth, you must identify the proper intervention and its role in managing change. Fifth, you need to test the results of interventions. If successful, the results will support the idea of applying the interventions to the entire organization. Finally, we discuss the importance of providing feedback to clients once an intervention has been selected and implemented.

Chapter Two

The Purpose of the Internal Consultant in an Ever-Changing Organization

THE PURPOSE OF THE INTERNAL CONSULTANT

One of the best ways to understand the *value* of internal consultants is to examine the purpose of HRD internal consultants.[1] There are eight fundamental purposes for consulting within an organization. We have listed these from the lowest to the highest influence on organizational change:

1. Providing information.
2. Solving problems.
3. Conducting an effective diagnosis.
4. Providing recommendations.
5. Implementing change.
6. Building consensus and commitment.
7. Facilitating client learning.
8. Improving organizational effectiveness.

The first five purposes are the ones most frequently requested by clients. They are often referred to as "traditional" purposes of consulting. The three remaining purposes require the most advanced skills of internal consultants. These skills include an understanding of the consulting process as well as establishing and managing the consultant/client relationship. It is important to remember that as an internal consultant you must first address the purposes the client requests and then direct your attention to other purposes.

1. Providing Information

The most common reason that an organization uses a consultant is for supplying special expertise or the most up-to-date information about a unique need of the organization. Organizational members may also request information about a training program, a human resource system, an instructional strategy, a needs analysis technique, or other research. In many instances, organizations may not be able to allocate enough human resources to get all of the information it needs. As a result, internal consultants are used to acquire and process the necessary information vital to the well-being of the organization.

Robert Dean, director of HRD at the Humana Corporation in Louisville, Kentucky, said that internal consultants in his organization, "serve as a clearinghouse for thousands of ideas each year. Without internal consultants at the Humana Corporation, vital data and research essential to improving performance and quality would not be available. The result would be that our organization would function far less efficiently than it does today."

2. Solving Problems

Many internal consultants spend much of their time helping organizations solve problems. A problem is defined as "the difference between what an organization has and what an organization wants." These problems may center around such things as communication, performance, quality, attitudes, and supervisory deficiencies.

One of the primary tasks of an internal consultant is to make sure that the problems identified by your client are indeed the ones that need to be solved. In other words, you must define the real issues and circumstances surrounding a problem. Then, you can build a clear and concise problem statement. Identifying the factors which contribute to a problem is an important step in problem-solving and a topic we discuss in Chapter 10.

3. Conducting an Effective Diagnosis

The third purpose of internal consulting is to effectively diagnose problems for the organization. In an interview with Charlene Seyfer of the Sandia Laboratories in Albuquerque, New Mexico, she stated that "the diagnosis phase of internal consulting is perhaps one of the most critical to improving organizational efficiency and effectiveness. It is during this phase that managers, supervisors, and executives become more actively involved in the consulting process. Their primary role is to provide access to information and their perspective of the current organizational environment."

To be successful, internal consultants must uncover and analyze a great deal of information. A complete diagnosis includes an external environmental analysis (i.e., economic condition and political and technical status of the organization) and an internal analysis (i.e., organizational structure, managerial abilities and attitudes, and organizational culture). (These analyses are discussed in Chapter 6.) The information you gather during this phase will help you make sound recommendations for change to the organization.

4. Providing Recommendations

You will make recommendations, including action items, based on what you have learned about the organization. Recommendations should be presented in a concise, logical, and step-by-step manner designed to improve the diagnosed problem.

The client then can decide how to carry out the recommendation. Internal consultants should also provide best and worst case scenarios for each recommendation to help the client make better selections among the recommendations.

5. Implementing Change

You should consider the following factors when implementing changes:

1. Changes must be chosen and designed to fit the organization. A tailored intervention is better for an organization

than the off-the-shelf approach that many internal consultants advocate.

2. Many changes can occur only after barriers are removed
   in the culture. Thus, it is your responsibility to identify
   barriers and obstacles before implementing changes.

3. There are certain points in the organization where
   changes are more likely to succeed.[2] They are referred to
   as *leverage points*. Internal consultants have the responsibility to introduce change at these leverage points to allow
   change to spread to the rest of the organization.

For example, some departments within an organization may
need more training activities than others (i.e., sales department,
customer service department). Therefore, internal consultants will
want to introduce change where it is more likely to be accepted.
This gives the proposed "change" an opportunity to be supported
by others in the organization.

Charles Butters, director of organizational planning with LTV
Corporation, believes that internal consultants must work closely
with managers, supervisors, and executives who are familiar with
the organization for change to be successful. He believes that this
group has the authority to bring about change. On the other hand,
implementing a change will often need specialized skills or knowledge that many managers, supervisors, and executives lack.

To carry out change, you must understand the potential outcomes and effects of your recommendations. Many internal consultants get this knowledge by observing similar recommendations
being implemented in other parts of the organization.

A combination of authority and experience can produce a partnership between the internal consultant and management, which
can empower both during the implementation phase. Without this
key partnership, change may not occur, nor will people be willing to do things differently, regardless of the possible positive
outcomes.

6. Building Consensus and Commitment

Wendy Lawson, director of executive development at Martin Marietta Corporation, said that when she works with executives, it is
essential to accomplish two things before building consensus and

commitment. First, you must establish trust between you and your client. Second, the organization must be ready to accept change. Both of these aims can be developed during the problem identification/diagnosis and recommendation phases of intervention consulting.

One way to decide the client's readiness for and commitment to change is by answering the following questions:[3]

1. How willing are the members of the organization to carry out change?
2. Is upper management willing to learn and use new management methods and practices?
3. What type of information do members of the organization readily accept or resist?
4. What are the members' attitudes toward change?
5. What are the executives' attitudes toward change?
6. How much do individual members of the organization regard their contribution to overall organizational effectiveness as a legitimate and desirable objective?

Another way to gauge readiness for change is to test the enthusiasm of clients for a particular recommendation. While it seems to be fairly straightforward, this gauge provides an instantaneous measure of resistance or resentment. Once you have figured out the level of enthusiasm, you may be able to encourage a certain recommendation.

7. Facilitating Client Learning

Ron Walker, executive vice president of William M. Mercer, Incorporated, said that "internal consultants can further facilitate learning by allowing clients to participate in the human resource development process."

The importance of facilitating client learning was very evident when he set up the International Professional Development Committee at Mercer, consisting of 14 senior members of the organization. Each of these individuals is responsible for the professional development activities within their region or country. This group meets four times a year to discuss the professional activities and performance improvement opportunities within the company. They engage in problem identification, diagnosis, and implementation of change interventions that bring about performance improvement and organizational effectiveness. Walker believes this committee can supply leadership by demonstrating the importance of lifelong learning.

Author Chris Argyris believes that one of the primary barriers to learning is that, "professionals are always successful at what they do; they rarely experience failure. Because they have rarely failed, they have never learned how to learn from failure."[4] Failure is one of the most enriching—although painful—learning experiences individuals can have. Internal consultants must help organizational leaders understand that trying new ideas or interventions that fail may well be the type of opportunities that provide the most enriching learning experiences, because failure forces you to reflect on your thoughts and feelings. This reflection enables you to better understand your behavior and actions, which gives you a frame of reference for future activities.

Traditionally, fostering client learning is a process of identifying needs and then designing and developing training interventions to address those needs. Monitoring and giving feedback after a training or change intervention has been carried out is perhaps the most important activity for an internal consultant.[5] These activities encourage coaching of new skills and providing reward or feedback processes that allow employees to continue to practice the skills after training.

8. Improving Organizational Effectiveness

The final purpose of the internal consulting process is to improve organizational effectiveness. It is the ability to adapt strategies and behaviors to future environmental change by maximizing contributions of the organization's human resources.[6]

Internal consultants must help decision-makers select the most appropriate interventions. Recommendations and solutions must be tailored to the organization's immediate and future problems. Simultaneously, internal consultants should try to overcome the obstacles that prevent change from occurring. Each of these activities enables top management to assure the organization's future existence in an ever-changing world.

"Organizational effectiveness implies that management is dedicated to the process of developing and maintaining the most important systems and linkages," according to Richard Chang, president of Chang and Associates. "Improving organizational effectiveness is the only reason internal HRD consultants should exist."

ACTIVITIES OF INTERNAL CONSULTANTS

Internal consultants have many responsibilities. They can be summed up best as eight primary activities:

1. Information specialist.
2. Fact-finder.
3. Trainer/educator.
4. Advocate.
5. Joint problem-solver.
6. Identifier of alternatives and linker to resources.
7. Process counselor.
8. Objective observer reflector.[7]

We overview each of the eight activities and then supply a matrix that shows the relationship among the eight activities and design, implementation, and performance management. We also give examples of how we have participated in each of the eight activities.

Information Specialist

As an information expert or technical specialist, the internal consultant is fulfilling the traditional role of consulting. You have the expert knowledge, skills, and professional experience that is so vital to the organization. Your primary responsibility is to provide information needed by individuals, groups, and the organization to help define problems and make decisions.

On several occasions, we have been invited to serve on conference design committees to provide information about the best ways to improve learning transfer. In addition, we have helped plan and design conference agendas and programs for senior consultants and managing directors. In this role, we act as a warehouse of training and conference design information that the committee can use.

Fact Finder

As a fact finder, you gather, analyze, and synthesize information the client needs to make a decision. You serve as a researcher. This activity requires a high level of competence in designing and developing formal survey instruments and in using several methods for gathering information. This often overlooked activity minimizes part of the problem-solving and decision-making process, and is, perhaps, one of the most critical activities of an internal consultant.

In this activity, we are generally designing, conducting, and analyzing learning needs and performance deficiencies. In one assignment, we worked with our *client relationships* practice to help identify the skills needed to effectively build and maintain client relationships. We worked with several consultants from throughout the United States to develop competency models that were used to help design and develop a training curriculum for client relationship managers.

Trainer/Educator

Internal consultants use stand-up training skills and techniques when performing this activity. You must have an understanding of the learning process and a comprehensive knowledge of the teaching/learning process, the appropriate use of instructional methods, understanding and application of experiential-learning activities, and excellent presentation, listening, and facilitating skills. When performing this activity, you may well be delivering training programs or interventions that improve performance and create organizational change. In some situations, you may simply recommend which learning processes are best to use.

One of our primary responsibilities is to conduct professional development activities to improve the skills of our consultants, which result in improved performance and organizational effectiveness. The professional development courses include: project and time management, interpersonal skills, sales training, listening skills, presentation skills, meeting management, team building and supervisory skills training. We spend approximately 25 percent of our time on this activity. It is important to note that the type of training conducted by our internal consultants is for midlevel and senior consultants, managing directors, and office heads. Other forms of training are conducted by less senior HRD professionals or outside training consulting firms.

Advocate

The *advocate* activity is the most directive. It requires you to influence the organization to choose particular goals or values that improve performance. Internal consultants may become more proactive and persuasive in performance-related issues. It could be said that internal consultants are ''selling organizational leaders'' during this activity.

Recently, we served as subject-matter experts to help our San Francisco, Denver, Pittsburgh, and Stamford offices set up project management standards. Our primary responsibilities were to help the operating committees of each office decide what standards were proper. We functioned much of the time as advocates for certain standards and supplied evidence and information about their value. This activity at Mercer resembles a philosopher and futurist. Positions and decisions advocated are based on both fact (evidence) and insight (guesses). The value of this activity is that it helps people with differing points of view resolve their conflicts.

Joint Problem-Solver

You must use a synergistic approach, collaborating with the client in a perceptual, cognitive, and action-taking process, to solve a problem during this activity.[8] This approach requires you to become an active participant in the problem-solving process. You must gently balance a directive and objective approach with the client to properly define existing problems and test alternatives for an effective resolution to the problem. You are acting in a partnership relationship during this activity. Focus your attention on identifying problems and evaluating, selecting, and carrying out alternatives. You must maintain a collaborative and participatory demeanor to approach the situation properly.

Our Los Angeles office asked us to facilitate a team-building session for its officers to identify problems and their solutions. We spent two days with this group analyzing the situation, examining their roles, and finding solutions. Finally, we spent the last three hours of the second day developing an action plan that all members would be willing to commit to. One result of our efforts was improved communication and better teamwork. The most important result was the creation of a senior advisory committee responsible for policy and operations decisions. During a feedback session, we discovered very positive results and improved morale and communication.

Alternative Identifier and Linker

During this activity, your primary responsibility is to find alternatives and resources for clients and help them assess consequences. You set up relative criteria for assessing the alternative, develop cause-and-effect relationships for each alternative, and establish a proper set of strategies. You are not directly involved in decision-making; the client is as proactive as you are.

This activity is often overlooked because it is one of the least formal of all of them. At Mercer, we may get 10–15 requests for resources each month. In many cases, the primary activity is a simple telephone conversation with the interested party to share the needed information. Joe Davidson, director of human resources in Mercer's central region, was asked by our Milwaukee office to find a special type of sales training for its consultants. He called us for help. We were able to determine the need and supply him with the names of five training programs conducted by outside vendors. He phoned each one to find out more information. Ultimately, he decided to use an in-house Mercer sales training course, which we helped change to meet his needs.

Process Counselor

As a process counselor, your primary responsibility is to help clients focus on and develop diagnostic skills to address specific performance problems, paying attention to *how* things are done rather than on *what tasks* are performed. During this activity, you begin to look at organizational structure, job design, work flow, performance appraisal and review, employee attitudes, performance criteria and standards, and quality improvement processes. This activity requires internal consultants to keep a high level of interpersonal and group skills to help performance improvement and organizational change. The primary goal of this activity is for employees to become more effective and improve performance.

We delivered a project management program to a select number of consultants in our Stamford, Connecticut, office. The officers were very pleased with the results and asked us to train the entire office. While we were delighted to provide the training, we felt that to achieve better results, we must design a comprehensive strategy to help improve performance and learning transfer.

We worked closely with Pat Daniels, director of human resources, to design the strategy, which included: (1) identifying problems, (2) identifying goals, (3) communicating with the senior consultant about participants' roles and responsibilities to help implement skills taught and remove barriers to skill transfer, (4) developing work-team classes, including support personnel, (5) scheduling the training program by breaking the course into three half-day sessions that helped participants immediately apply the skills taught, (6) conducting the training, (7) designing a performance feedback process to provide positive reinforcement of new skills, (8) developing follow-up activities, training aids, and forms to improve implementation, and (9) conducting refresher courses three months after the original training program.

Objective Observer/Reflector

During this activity, you are a philosopher and a verifier. Your primary responsibility is to ask reflective questions and help the clients clarify, modify, and alter a given situation. Asking reflective questions is very important during the implementation of quality

FIGURE 2–1
Matrix of Internal Consultant Roles with Activities

Designer	Information Specialist
	Fact-Finder
Implementor	Trainer/Educator
Performance Manager	Advocate
	Joint Problem-Solver
	Identifier of Alternatives and
	Resources
Process Consultant	Process Counselor
	Objective Observer

improvement processes, identification of performance standards, use of effective performance appraisal and review processes, implementation of job design and redesign activities, and other organizational change interventions. This is a nondirective activity because you guide the client to overcome barriers that prevent appropriate performance improvement.

We observed a training program in San Francisco designed to improve client interactions. The program was conducted by Bob Brinkerhoff of Western Michigan University. The purpose of observing the program was to help us develop follow-up strategies and training aids and to identify opportunities for applying the skills taught. We discovered where and when the skills taught could be used best. This observation helped us design a refresher course (conducted three months after the original training), training aids (a communication planner), and a performance feedback strategy used throughout the year and during performance appraisals.

In Figure 2–1, we have provided a matrix that reflects the relationship between the eight activities and the design, implementation, and performance management process. The most indirect activities are involved in the design process because they have less of a direct impact on performance improvement and organizational effectiveness.

Internal consultants become more directive as they move from implementor to performance management specialist. This latter role is a major focus for internal consultants.

FIGURE 2–2
Types of Organizations

Source: Eric H. Neilsen, *Becoming An OD Practitioner,* © 1984, p.17. Adapted by permission of Prentice Hall, Englewood Cliffs, New Jersey.

TYPES OF ORGANIZATIONS

The success of internal consultants is largely based on the type of organization with which they interact. There are four types of organizations relative to how management sees its employees and the relationship of the employees to the organization (see Figure 2-2):[9]

- Passive.
- Hierarchial.
- Competitive.
- Collaborative.

Passive Organizations

In passive organizations, employees are not viewed as important, and they are not perceived to be committed to the welfare of the organization. This type of organization does not rely on the talents, abilities, and skills of its employees to solve problems or to make essential contributions. The philosophy toward human resources in this type of organization is that of a revolving door; an attitude that internal human resources are easily replaced by others outside the organization. This orientation may not be conducive to the kinds of activities internal consultants can provide. **If internal consultants are involved in such an organization, their primary responsibility is to alter the passive attitude of management toward its employees.**

Hierarchial Organizations

In hierarchial organizations, employees are viewed as committed to the welfare of the organization, but only a few have important talents, abilities, or skills to offer. As a result, the organization is often a tall hierarchial one with many layers of management. Those layers closest to the bottom of the hierarchy are not seen as being very critical to reaching the ultimate goal of the organization. **The primary focus of internal consultants in this situation is the top 30 percent of the organization.** Internal consulting activities are not appropriate on a systemwide basis because all employees are not seen as critical to the outcome of the organization.

Competitive Organizations

Competitive organizations consist of many talented and skilled employees. Only a few however, are loyal to the organization. In many cases, the employees have a high level of education, many years of experience, and specialized talents and abilities. Most are able to find employment in a number of other competitive firms. This threat places extreme pressure on management and organizational leaders to keep their employees. **One of the principal activities of internal consultants in this type of organization is to focus management's attention on helping employees become actively involved in the operation of the organization.** Therefore, internal consultants in this type of organization help improve the organizational loyalty and commitment of employees.

Collaborative Organizations

Collaborative organizations allow their employees to participate in most, if not all, aspects of the organization. They see employees as important and committed to the welfare of the organization. The organizational culture fosters loyalty and involvement as well as participation. Internal consulting is a process that is encouraged and supported by upper management. **One of the principal outcomes of internal consulting in this type of organization is to develop a culture that uses employees' talents, abilities, and skills, and encourages commitment.** This type of organization is often viewed as a partnership relationship between management and employees. In many cases, this type of organization has the greatest potential for improving organizational efficiency.

The type of organization you are a part of will help you figure out management's attitude toward human resources. Management's attitude toward human resources will help you identify the evolutionary phase of your HRD program, described below.

THE EVOLUTION OF HRD: SIX PHASES

Human resource development in organizations can consist of one of six phases (see Figure 2–3):

1. No HRD.
2. One-person HRD program.
3. Vendor-driven HRD.
4. Vendor/customized HRD.
5. Organizationally-focused HRD.
6. Performance-centered HRD.

In some organizations, HRD has evolved from little or no involvement by part of management to becoming a strategic focus of the organization. In today's modern organization, any one of these six phases may exist.

1. No HRD

At Rhoden Nissan in Lincoln, Nebraska, Patrick Combs, general sales manager, said there is no HRD program within its six-store chain of automobile dealerships. As a result, little or no training

FIGURE 2-3
Evolution of HRD within an Organization

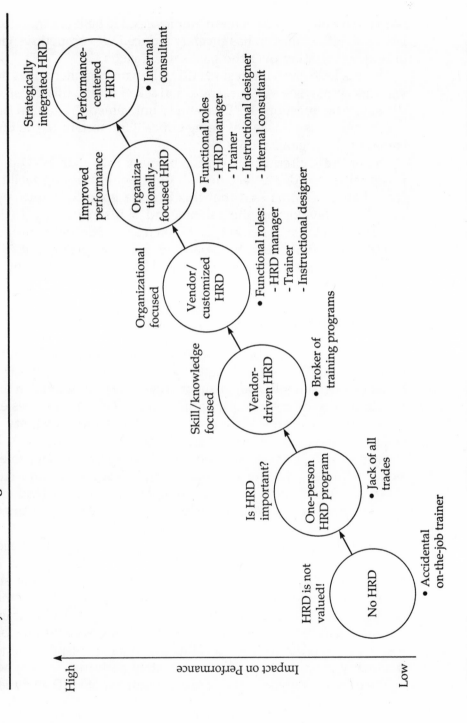

is given to new hires or veteran employees. He believes that "the lack of an HRD function has severely reduced the competitiveness of our organization over the past several years."

There is little or no interest in HRD when management does not value its employees. A typical question asked during this phase is, "What is the question? HRD is simply not valued." HRD, in this circumstance, is not seen as being critically important to the outcomes of the organization.

Under these circumstances, the primary role of an HRD professional is that of an "accidental, on-the-job, training facilitator." Patrick Combs said that this is not a good long-term approach to developing the talents and skills necessary to be successful in today's marketplace. Such an accidental approach to HRD does not mean that training does not occur, but it is generally haphazard, inconsistent, and not focused on organizational improvement.

2. One-Person HRD Program

Doug Smith, associate professor, Florida International University, shared with us that the most difficult type of HRD function is that of the one-person HRD department. The HRD professional in this situation must be a generalist of the highest level. This places extreme pressure on the HRD practitioner to perform a variety of skills and tasks, sometimes at a moderate level of efficiency. In many cases, the individuals who serve in this role are not professionally trained, but are line managers, salespersons, and customer service agents who do an exemplary job in their field and then are promoted to the training function because of their content expertise.

Under this circumstance, one person is responsible for needs assessment, design, and development and implementation of training and change interventions in the organization. He or she is also responsible for evaluating such programs to decide whether or not learning has occurred, behavior has changed, and/or training has had a positive effect on the organization. These responsibilities are a tall order for a single HRD practitioner; responsibilities that many practitioners cannot adequately perform.

The primary question asked during this phase of HRD evolution is, "Is training important to the organization?" It is a question often left unanswered. Why? Because management is using limited resources to demonstrate that their human resources are critical to the outcome of the organization. Management's commitment to HRD is very weak, which diminishes the importance of HRD in the organization. Therefore, employees are skeptical about HRD programs.

The primary role of HRD practitioners during this phase is that of the jack-of-all-trades. As described previously, HRD professionals are analysts, designers, developers, trainers, and evaluators, all rolled into one. Because each of these roles is complex and complicated, each could be a function in and of itself. But since one practitioner does it all, this approach may severely impact the quality of the HRD function within the organization. Therefore, the HRD practitioner may not be seen by fellow employees as credible or "truly professional."

3. Vendor-Driven HRD

As HRD begins to emerge from the one-person HRD program to a smattering of a few HRD practitioners, it is often referred to as the *vendor-driven HRD program*. The primary focus of this type of program is to find outside training programs that can be used within the organization. There is little or no effort made to customize the programs to fit the organizational culture. The purpose is simply to deliver training to as many people as possible.

This approach is often referred to as the "activity strategy" of HRD.[10] The focus is on keeping an accurate count of the number of individuals who attend training during the year.

Jane McGee, director of HRD at Lincoln Telephone Company in Lincoln, Nebraska, recently described this type of HRD function. She believes the vendor-driven HRD program can indeed change organizational efficiency. She says that, "If vendor programs are properly selected, based on the needs of the organization and its employees, this strategy can be a very effective one."

During this phase, one of the critical questions asked by HRD professionals is, "What skills or knowledge are lacking among employees?" This question is a much more sophisticated one than any other previously asked because the focus is on skills and knowledge that impact performance. Even though this question does not directly focus on improving organizational effectiveness, it is moving in the right direction for HRD practitioners.

When an HRD program is in this phase, the HRD practitioners primarily serve as a clearinghouse of vendor programs. Their job is to identify programs that appear to be most closely aligned with developing the skills and knowledge needed to perform given tasks and/or jobs. They are known as a *broker* of training programs.

In many instances, the choice of training programs can produce a positive outcome for organizations. Training and change interventions that are designed specifically for an organization to improve performance and quality, however, have greater potential for improving organizational effectiveness.

4. Vendor/Customized HRD Programs

The next phase of evolution of HRD is similar to that of the previous one. The primary difference is that the HRD practitioners are making an effort to customize programs to more closely align with the organization's environment and culture. This plan is often referred to as *customizing vendor programs.*

During this phase, "pure" instructional design activities emerge. In other words, HRD practitioners are responsible for completely designing and developing training programs. This includes conducting a formal needs assessment, designing and developing the activities, and carrying out the programs on-site. This phase of HRD is best referred to as a hybrid consisting of outside vendor programs and customized programs designed by internal staffs.

During this phase, the primary question being asked of HRD professionals is, "How can training become more organizationally focused?" In many cases, this question is not being asked by the HRD professionals but by the organization's management. As a result, HRD practitioners are responding to management's pressure to customize their training programs for the organization. This pressure helps explain why "formal" instructional design is becoming an increasingly important HRD activity.

Gloria Regalbuto, president of Seacorp University, a division of

Seacorp Bank in Seattle, said, "HRD programs which are in this vendor/customized phase are beginning to examine the critical issues facing the organization."

She also adds that, "the amount of resources committed to customizing HRD programs will greatly determine whether or not the HRD function remains in this phase or evolves to a higher level."

During this phase of evolution, three of the four HRD functional roles begin to emerge: HRD manager, trainer, and instructional designer. Trainers and HRD managers are becoming more specialized during this phase, while the role of instructional designer is just beginning.

One way to decide whether or not an organization is in the fourth phase of evolution is to discover if job titles or descriptions separate the practitioners into distinct roles. If they do, the HRD function has entered this phase of evolution.

5. Organizationally-Focused HRD

It is during this phase that HRD becomes a strategic weapon in the organization. Bud Baskin, senior HRD professional with Arthur Anderson & Co., believes that HRD programs in this phase are indeed focusing on performance improvement and quality for the particular organization. Vendor programs are no longer used.

Instructional designers are feverishly working in the back rooms of organizations designing and developing programs that are organizationally focused. Gone are the days of purchasing an outside program, changing it a bit, and then delivering it. It is during this phase that organizations begin to demand much more of HRD professionals and hold them accountable for a much higher level of performance. This accountability requires a greater competency and skill by HRD practitioners.

During this phase, HRD practitioners are asked the following question, "How can HRD improve employee performance in our organization?"

Evaluation becomes increasingly important during this phase. The focus of evaluation is no longer on whether or not employees enjoyed the training activity, but on whether or not HRD interventions improve behavior and have a positive impact on the organization's profitability and effectiveness. If HRD professionals cannot show such improvements, the function will not be supported financially by organizational leaders.

At this phase of development, the HRD function is seen by upper management as an investment in bottom-line results. HRD practitioners must answer this call by supplying programs that indeed improve performance, quality, and efficiency of the organization.

During phase five of the evolution, the primary role of HRD professionals includes four functional roles: HRD manager, trainer, instructional designer, and internal consultant.[11]

The HRD managers, trainers, and instructional designers function similarly in this phase as they did in the vendor/customized HRD program phase. The primary difference is that instructional designers are much more highly trained and skilled professionals. It is not unusual for all HRD professionals in this phase to have masters and doctorate degrees.

The internal consultant role is a newly identified role during this phase. The consultant primarily focuses on the first five purposes of consulting previously discussed: providing information, solving problems, conducting effective diagnoses, supplying recommendations, and implementing changes.

6. Performance-Centered HRD

This phase of evolution is very similar to the previous one. The primary difference is that HRD programs are focused exclusively on performance improvement and organizational effectiveness. It is not enough for HRD to be organizationally-focused. It must improve the organization's ability to compete. Wendy Lawson, Martin Marietta Corporation, echoed this belief when she stated that, "executives have little or no patience with HRD programs that are not performance-centered."

It is during this phase that organizations spend large portions of their HRD resources on up-front analysis and evaluation. These types of activities need a great deal of involvement by internal consultants.

Internal consultants within the organization are asked to answer the question, "How can HRD be strategically integrated into the organizational culture to improve organizational effectiveness and employee performance?''

This question helps us show why analysis and evaluation have become paramount in the organization. Much of the energy spent by internal consultants is to document the impact of HRD programs on the organization. This type of effort is being demanded by upper management to justify the financial expenditure on HRD.

During this phase, the internal consultant role has fully emerged within the organization. The job description of internal consultants here is one of a strategic partner in improving performance and organizational efficiency. Their primary focus should be on building consensus and commitment, facilitating client learning, and improving organizational effectiveness.

Chapter Three

Using the Analysis Phase of HRD to Improve Organizational Effectiveness

The first HRD process for internal consultants is "analysis" so you can determine current performance and contrast that with the desired performance. The difference between these states supplies critical information when you are choosing corrective actions to improve the skills, knowledge, and attitudes of employees. Ultimately, these improvements should enhance the efficiency of the individual as well as the organization.

LEARNING TO ASK WHY

Consider the following scenario: You're sitting at your desk late Wednesday afternoon, and your phone rings. You pick it up. It's the executive vice president of marketing. He states in no uncertain terms that he is disappointed in his sales staff's ability to make cold calls and do proper client prospecting. He continues to tell you that he is feeling a lot of pressure from the president to generate revenue during the last two quarters of the year so the company can meet a fairly aggressive budget.

He then asks if you can develop a two-day sales training program on cold calls and client prospecting. He asks you how much time it would take for your staff to design such a program and have it available for delivery to his staff. He is anxious to get this program started within the next three or four weeks. He says he will get back with you in a couple of days to finalize plans for designing and developing this short sales training program. After hanging up the phone, you slump back in your chair and think, "What do I do now?"

For many, a request for training from a senior member of the organization is a "reason" for immediate action. Many would assemble their staffs, set up the parameters of the project, establish time lines, identify available resources, put together a project schedule and start acting. But is that the correct decision?

All too often, internal consultants react before thinking. In the analysis phase, your primary job is to consider what possibilities, circumstances, events, and conditions are causing a performance problem. In addition, has management communicated to its staffs its desired intentions for them? Have they communicated the performance they want and identified the performance standards its staffs will be measured against? Other possible questions might be: Is this a performance problem? Is this a condition of the environment? Do employees understand their role? Is the performance a failure to have the activity performed, or is it a skill deficiency?

In situations like this one, internal consultants have an obligation to figure out *why* a program is needed. You should think before reacting. In many circumstances, supplying a training program such as the one in the example may solve the problem, but it may not be the most appropriate intervention.

For example, let's suppose the internal consultant accepted the responsibility to design the requested sales training program and it failed to improve the performance of the sales staff. At that point, the vice president of marketing may well point an accusing finger at the internal consultant and the training activity. Then, the credibility of the internal consultant and the HRD program is in question. The HRD group could well be locked into a battle of defending itself against the senior member of the management team.

Simply failing to ask difficult questions early can create a scenario that may ultimately produce negative results for you and the HRD program. *The solution is to think analytically.* Continually ask about the organization and its financial and competitive position, its strengths and weaknesses, its management structure, its management capacity, its technological state, its relationship to competitors, its reward and compensation system used to motivate employees, its performance appraisal and performance review systems, and management's attitude toward human resources within the organization.

By constantly exploring these issues, internal consultants are not focused on the status quo but on continuously looking for new and improved ways of enhancing the efficiency of the organization. Therefore, analysis is as much a state of mind as it is a series of techniques and processes. Internal consultants who are always inquiring are ones constantly in touch with the problems facing the organization.

FIVE CRITICAL QUESTIONS

To effectively use the analysis process, you should consider answering the following five questions:

1. What is the definition of a problem?
2. Where is the "pain?"
3. What evidence do you have to support your point of view or perspective?
4. What does the organizational leadership prefer to do?
5. How should you best proceed?

Figure 3–1 illustrates how to analyze performance problems.

"What is the Definition of a Problem?"

One of the sources of confusion about analysis is the lack of a generally accepted, useful, and substantive definition of a problem. It's useful to think of a problem as a gap between a current set of circumstances and some changed or desired set of circumstances. In other words, a problem is the difference between "what is" and "what should be."

In an HRD setting, proficiencies (knowledge, skills, attitudes), performance, or situations describe these circumstances. Problems could also deal with desires, interests, or deficiencies. Achieving the changed or desired set of circumstances can be described as altering the current situation. The most common

FIGURE 3–1
Analyzing Performance Problems

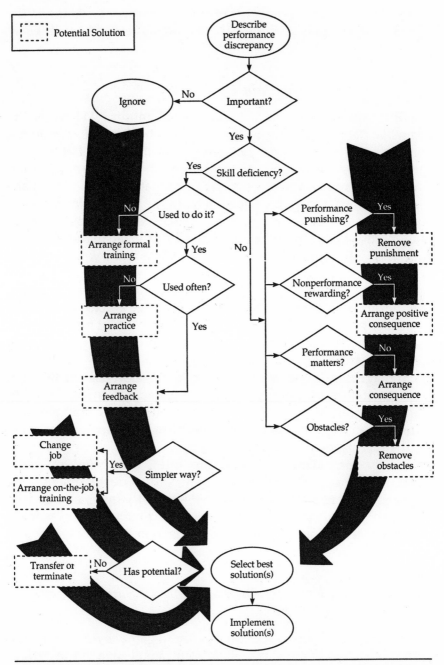

Excerpted from: R. Mager and P. Pipe, *Analyzing Performance Problems*, 2d ed. (Belmont, Calif.: Lake Publishing Company, 1984).

forms of alterations are training programs and interventions that are planned, designed, and developed by internal consultants.

"Where is the Pain?"

Another question facing internal consultants is "Where is the pain?" or "the gap?" The analysis process begins with identifying the type of gap confronting internal consultants and HRD.[1] Each gap has its own methods and techniques for reducing or eliminating the difference between what is and what should be. The gaps are (1) performance gaps, deficiencies in the way employees carry out their assignments and duties; (2) management gaps, deficiencies in the way people are managed and motivated in the organization; and (3) organizational gaps, deficiencies in the way an organization is conceived and designed.

Performance gaps are usually reduced through training activities designed to give new skills and knowledge and to improve the attitudes of employees. Then, employees can adopt new methods of performance that are more in line with the desired performance of the organization.

Management gaps, on the other hand, are reduced through changes in management practices and techniques. Internal consultants can often be used to show these practices and techniques and supply training programs to end performance gaps of managers and supervisors.

Finally, **organizational gaps** are often eliminated by redesigning the organization using organizational development techniques and practices. Once again, internal consultants can be used to provide these techniques and practices, and supply an internal perspective of the organization, its problems, and practices.

"What Evidence Do You Have To Support Your Point of View?"

There are some techniques you can use to gather evidence to support your point of view as well as your perspective of the current and the desired state. They include:

1. Focus groups.
2. Interviews.
3. Questionnaires.
4. Observation.

Gathering input about the needs of an organization is important so you are not operating in a vacuum of your own thoughts or the thoughts of management. Gathering input from employees is critical to finding the training needs of your client.

Focus Groups—what they are. Focus groups are small discussion groups of a few employees, led by a facilitator. The purpose is to focus on a topic and get an in-depth look at the focus group's opinions about the topic. Sometimes this activity means educating the group first, then discussing their opinions. Other times, the attendees already know the topic; they simply answer questions that elicit their feedback on the topic or that ask for their recommendations for change.

Why do them. Focus groups give you the opportunity to get in-depth information about a group's opinions. With focus groups, you can ask follow-up questions to find out "why" as well as "what" the group thinks.

The other way to get in-depth information is through interviews (discussed below). However, a person may hesitate to give as much detail in an individual interview as he would in the comfort of a focus group with other people. On the other hand, sometimes the groundswell of opinion of a few in the group can sway the opinion of other group members, tainting the true feelings of the group.

To alleviate this problem, sometimes facilitators have focus group members complete a brief questionnaire before the discussion begins. The facilitator then collects the questionnaire and uses this information to balance against what the group said. Occasionally, the two pieces of information differ because of group dynamics and peer pressure.

Other feedback mechanisms, such as questionnaires and observations, give the "what" but not the "why" that focus groups provide. These techniques are discussed later in this chapter.

Makeup of the group. Ideally, focus groups should be limited to 10 people, plus a facilitator and note-taker. The 10 people generally should be a random sample and should represent a cross-section of one strata of the organization. Senior and junior levels should not be mixed because the junior-level attendee may not participate fully if a senior-level person is also in the room. That's why members of management should not sit in to "listen" to what the group says, unless it is a group of their peers.

Since each group includes only 10 people, it is best to conduct several focus groups so you get the opinion of a greater number of people. You will never, however, get the opinion of all people using focus groups. Questionnaires are best used for that purpose and discussed later in this chapter.

The internal consultant acts as the facilitator in focus groups. This role requires that you ask pertinent questions to find out what opinions, needs, and concerns the members of the group have. Simply asking the question, "What kind of training do you need?" will not give you the information you're looking for. Instead, you could describe various situations and ask the members of the focus group for their opinions about that situation or how to handle it. Their answers will tell you which skills they are lacking.

Logistics. The best location for focus groups is in a private room with a door so outsiders cannot hear what is going on. Focus group members will feel more comfortable about speaking freely if they have privacy.

If at all possible, conduct focus groups on company time. If you have shift workers who cannot attend during working hours, pay them overtime to attend right before their shift, if possible. The attendance and attention span is much better when employees are being paid to participate.

The best length of time for focus groups generally is no more than an hour and one half. Any longer time becomes boring for the participants, may turn the session into a "bitch session," and takes the attendees away from their work for too long. If you cannot cover all of the topics in this period, plan to conduct follow-up sessions.

Always tell focus group participants what the purpose of the group is—that is, what you want to know from them. When you start by giving them this information, they will understand why you are asking their opinion and will be more likely to tell you their true feelings. Also, tell them what you plan to do with the information you gather.

Obviously, it helps if you have already established credibility with members of the group. If you don't know most or any of the members, spend a few minutes giving them some background about yourself and warming up to them.

Interviews. Another technique for gathering input is to conduct one-on-one interviews with employees, managers, and supervisors. As with any interviewing process, interviews about HRD and training needs allow you to focus your attention on the opinions of one person at a time. You can find out the "why" behind a person's statement in an interview, but you run the risk of having them hold back some information because they feel they are out there alone with their opinion.

As stated earlier, the dynamics of a focus group may encourage some people to voice their opinions more readily if they feel that others in the group share their opinion. With an individual interview, the person you're talking with **may** not be as willing to share his or her thoughts. However, the opposite can be true, since there is no one else listening except you.

Managers and supervisors often feel more comfortable giving their opinions in interviews instead of focus groups. Even if the group is made up of their peers, managers often prefer to voice their opinions about organizational change in a more private setting. It is also easier to schedule the time of one manager instead of a group of managers at once. Therefore, interviews often work best for this group.

Questionnaires. A questionnaire is one means of eliciting the thoughts, feelings, beliefs, experiences, and attitudes of employees, managers, supervisors, and executives. It is a concise, preplanned set of questions, designed to yield specific information about a particular topic.[2]

Questionnaires should be used only after all other sources of information on the topic have been thoroughly researched and you have specific areas to explore. Questionnaires succeed or fail based on the questions they ask; the more specific the question, the more valuable the answer.

Surveys (questionnaires) are a good way to get information from a large group of people. If a survey is sent to a group or all employees in an organization and your response rate is high (70 percent or more), you are getting feedback from many more people than you would get through focus groups or interviews.

Getting a high response rate is difficult unless completing the survey is mandatory. However, even at that, you will never collect surveys from everyone. To get a high response rate on a voluntary survey, the following items are important:

- Keep the survey as brief as possible. Even if you have 30 questions to ask, group the questions so you can number them 1a, 1b, 1c, instead of 1, 2, and 3. This arrangement will make the questionnaire appear shorter.
- Limit the number of open-ended questions; use primarily ranking questions (rank from 1 through . . .), rating questions (show your level of agreement using a scale of 1 through 5), or multiple choice or yes/no questions. This arrangement makes it easier for the respondent to quickly complete the questionnaire.
- Keep the survey anonymous. You may gather demographic information on the questionnaire, but don't make the information so specific that individuals in a department can be identified.
- Provide an easy return method, either including a return envelope or giving instructions to place the questionnaire in some easily accessible location.
- Get a sponsor, if possible. Recipients are more likely to answer a questionnaire if a prestigious person, organization, or institution endorses the project.
- Choose the sample carefully. Questionnaires should be sent only to those who have the desired information and who are likely to be sufficiently interested to respond conscientiously and objectively.

Characteristics of a good questionnaire. Effective questionnaires should meet the following characteristics:

- Deals with a significant topic—a topic that individuals in the sample recognize as important enough to allow for the time needed for completing the questionnaire. The significance should be clearly stated on the questionnaire or in an accompanying letter.

- Is attractive in appearance, neatly and logically arranged, and clearly printed.
- Contains clear and complete directions and definitions of necessary terms, and is concise.
- Is objective, with no leading questions—questions that signal the response desired.
- Is logical and goes from general to specific responses.
- Is easy to tabulate and interpret. Tabulation sheets should be preconstructed, showing how the data will be handled *before* the final form of the questionnaire is decided.
- Includes a cover letter explaining the purpose of the questionnaire and any deadlines for responses.

Writing a questionnaire is a very difficult process. A single word can dramatically affect the information received. Keep in mind the following rules for properly constructing a questionnaire:

- Define or qualify terms that could be easily misunderstood or misinterpreted.
- Watch for descriptive adjectives and adverbs without an agreed-upon meaning such as frequently, occasionally, and rarely.
- Beware of double negatives. A respondent must study these carefully to answer properly.
- Underline a word if you want to emphasize it.
- Give a point of reference when asking for a rating.
- Avoid uncalled for assumptions.
- Phrase questions so they are appropriate for all respondents.
- Design questions that give complete possibilities for comprehensive responses.
- Provide for a systematic quantification of responses.

Observations. Internal consultants can collect data by watching one or more persons performing a series of skills. This activity is known as the *observation* method. Observation is used when detailed information is needed or when acquired skills need to be measured for accuracy and effectiveness. Observation can also measure personal traits such as self-control, cooperativeness, truthfulness, and honesty. Observation is appropriate only when job activities are observable, detailed information is needed, and the incumbent cannot supply the information.

Observation is, perhaps, most useful in deciding or setting standards for job tasks. When making observations, internal consultants must:

- Identify the person being watched and what the job function is.
- Describe the procedures being studied in sufficient detail to allow persons with no knowledge of the activity to follow the resulting instruction.
- Outline the order in which the task is completed.
- List any forms used in carrying out the task.
- Identify decision points and make a decision tree showing any alternatives resulting from those decisions.
- Pinpoint the circumstances under which the task takes place.
- Choose the best time for observation.
- Prepare a checklist, if one is used.
- Compare performance with existing standards.

Observations can either be structured or unstructured. *Structured observations* are those where you set up the observed performance in advance. Usually, internal consultants use checklists of the activities they expect to see to decide if the activity has been completed correctly. The checklist contains a list of each task in the order in which it is done to complete the activity. The results are used to show which tasks are done correctly and incorrectly.

Unstructured observations do not involve predetermined activities. Instead, you write down the tasks performed. The descriptions can include opinions and general information about the performance and the performer. Most of the "evidence" is anecdotal.

The internal consultant and the person under observation should not interact during the exercise. The internal consultant needs to be familiar enough with the task to recognize if the performance meets existing standards. You should however, be impartial.

Observers could include internal consultants, course developers, instructors, subject-matter experts, immediate supervisors, end-user personnel, and paid consultants.

"What Does the Organizational Leadership Prefer?"

Because internal consultants exist within a political environment, it is critical to always consider the current perspective and preferences of the senior management and organizational leaders. This consideration can prevent serious blunders such as making recommendations that are contrary to the current organizational culture and political views of key members of the organization. Checking management's view is also a way of verifying information discovered during analysis, before you make recommendations that oppose management's views.

It is not our intent to reduce the importance of research and analysis, but we want to caution you that it may alarm many organizational leaders. Examining the status quo and making recommendations to reach a different desired state is threatening to many people. Therefore, it is prudent for internal consultants to consider the organization's political climate, management's concerns, and management's willingness to listen to divergent points of view from individuals outside the inner circle.

"How Should You Best Proceed?"

Internal consultants often struggle with how best to proceed in the analysis phase of HRD. Before you decide how to go on, consider three critical principles of change: congruence, predisposition, and succession.[3] These are simple and straightforward concepts that you should consider before conducting any form of analysis.

The principle of *congruence* means that the intervention must be chosen, designed, and varied to fit the structure and function of the organization. This principle implies that a tailored analysis is better suited for an organization than the off-the-shelf approach.

The principle of *predisposition* says that there are certain points

---

Example

Recently, an HRD internal consultant recommended to his organization (a Fortune 1000 company) to outplace a majority of their training activities. His justification was based on an analysis of cost-containment and improved program flexibility. He used an external consulting firm to conduct the analysis and make recommendations.

The recommendation was received coolly by senior management because the chairman believed the organization had become too impersonal and distant. In fact, senior management was currently conducting its own analysis of how the organization could become more responsive to its employees and re-establish a "family" atmosphere.

The internal consultant's lack of awareness of the "shift in cultural emphasis" severely diminished his effectiveness within the organization. This tactical error resulted in a loss of credibility and created a perception that the HRD internal consultant was out of step with the rest of the organization. The proposal was disregarded and the internal consultant was told to align himself with the values of the organization.

It's obvious from this example that failure to account for the preferences of organizational leaders can severely impact your effectiveness and credibility. You should always check out current organizational biases before you make recommendations or suggestions. This awareness should help decrease embarrassing situations and outcomes.

---

in the organization where analyses are most likely to succeed. For example, a research department may be more receptive to analysis than another department because a researcher's job is to analyze. Analysis should be introduced at these "penetration points" or "leverage points" and be allowed to spread to the rest of the organization.[4]

The principle of *succession* holds that analysis is done indirectly, not directly, by a process where some things are changed to change other things. In other words, some changes can only occur after barriers and obstacles are removed in the culture, for example, reassuring employees and managers that the information shared will remain confidential.

Once you have considered these three principles of analysis, you must consider how to rank your analysis activities—which are most important and, at the same time, most urgent. These activities are your highest priorities. Analyses that are important, but not urgent, can be postponed until they become more urgent. Analyses that are perceived to be urgent, but not important, are often referred to as routine and should be treated as such. Since you have only a limited amount of time and resources to conduct analyses, you should consider only the analyses that have the greatest impact on the organization's effectiveness, efficiency, and quality.

We have included an Analysis Checklist at the end of this chapter to help you document your analysis.

TYPES OF ANALYSIS

Too often, training programs and interventions are developed in organizations simply because management perceives that a problem exists. In many cases, little attention is given to the *reasons why* training should be offered as a solution to organizational difficulties.

To understand *why* training should be offered, you should conduct one of three types of analysis to figure out how you should proceed. The simplest type of analysis is task analysis, followed by performance analysis and organizational analysis.

Task Analysis

Task analysis is a simple, straightforward process that names all of the steps needed to do a job. It is a type of blueprint or schematic that can be used to analyze performance at a micro level. It can also be used to supply detailed technical training for individuals entering a new job classification.

Perhaps the best way to conduct a task analysis is to assemble a group of exemplary employees and have them analyze their present job responsibilities. This analysis includes all tasks they do to complete the job. Once all the tasks have been named, participants should show the proper sequence of tasks. Employees should also identify the resources necessary to do the job and the conditions

Example

Several years ago, the CEO of a major research hospital was very concerned about shrinking market share. While attending a national medical conference, he attended a seminar about customer service quality and its impact on revenue growth. He left the seminar concerned that poor telephone service was one of the reasons for the hospital's shrinking market share. He immediately requested that the HRD department design and deliver a training program that would improve telephone-answering response time and service quality. He further insisted that all employees, including physicians, nursing staff, office personnel, and custodial employees, participate in the training.

The director of HRD, unconvinced that telephone training was the best strategy to improve the market-share problem, decided to conduct a comprehensive analysis of the situation. She wanted to make certain that the training program was going to improve the quality of telephone service and address the problem of shrinking market share.

Her staff quickly developed an analysis strategy, which included telephone interviews with former patients, face-to-face interviews with staff members, a questionnaire designed to determine the current perceptions of telephone service, and a formal observation of telephone-answering response time and the communication skills used during telephone conversations.

The conclusions of the analysis were very different from the perspective of the CEO. First, more than 75 percent of former patients felt telephone service at the hospital was very satisfactory. Staff members maintained a similar perception. Information from the questionnaire showed problems with telephone response time, although the quality of service was very good. The formal observation activities uncovered a similar finding.

The reason was the number of telephones available on many of the floors was wholly inadequate. In addition, the number of telephone lines available was not sufficient for the volume of calls received. The conclusion was that quality of telephone service was not a result of a skill or performance deficiency, but a result of an inadequate telephone system.

The director of HRD presented these findings to her boss, the vice president of human resources, who passed it on to the CEO. After an initial negative reaction, "Why didn't you follow my

---

Example (Continued)

explicit instruction?'' he was delighted with the findings. He made funding available for a new telephone system, which included operations and skills training. In addition, he agreed that a formal market analysis was needed to provide answers to the market share problem.

He was so impressed with the results of the analysis conducted by the HRD department that he asked the director to work with the marketing department to design a market analysis strategy. Simply by "thinking" before reacting, the internal consultant prevented inappropriate, unnecessary training that would not improve the situation.

---

and types of support necessary to adequately do it. Tasks should then be ranked. As an internal consultant, you should also ask for input about the types of training activities needed to best train an individual in this type of job.

Performance Analysis

The second type of analysis helps find the cause(s) of performance deficiencies. Internal consultants should first examine the employees' current level of skill and knowledge and measure their attitudes. Then, compare this information with the required level of skill and knowledge. The difference between the two is the basis for future training programs and interventions.

You can use the following performance analysis model to answer 12 questions about performance:[5]

1. What is the performance discrepancy?
   a. What is the difference between what is being done and what is expected?
   b. What is your evidence?
   c. How reliable is your evidence?
2. Is the discrepancy important?
   a. Why?
   b. What happens if we do nothing?

    c. Is it worth making better?
3. Is it a lack of skill?
    a. Could the performers do the job if their lives depended on doing it correctly?
    b. Are present skills at least adequate?
4. Were they able to perform successfully in the past?
    a. Have they forgotten?
    b. Do they know it's still expected of them?
5. Is the needed skill used frequently?
    a. Do they get regular feedback on how they are or are not doing?
    b. Exactly how do they find out how they are doing?
    c. How do they view the way they are told?
6. Is there a similar way to do the job?
    a. Would job descriptions clear up the problem?
    b. Can they learn/relearn by watching others?
    c. Can the job be changed in some way?
7. Do they have what it takes to do the job?
    a. Is the physical and/or mental potential there?
    b. Are they qualified?
8. Is the desired performance evidently being punished?
    a. What is in it for the performer to do it right?
    b. Is doing it somehow self-punishing?
    c. Is there some pressure not to perform?
9. Is not doing the job rewarded in some way?
    a. Is there some reward for doing it wrong?
    b. Does doing it wrong draw attention?
    c. What rewards the wrong performance now?
    d. Do performers worry less or get less tired if they do less work?
10. Does doing the job right really matter?
    a. Is there a favorable outcome for doing?
    b. Is there an unfavorable outcome for not doing?
    c. Is there pride in doing?
    d. Not doing?
    e. Is there any status or lack of it connected with the job?
11. Are there obstacles to performing?
    a. Do they know what is expected?
    b. Do they know when it is expected?

    c. Are there too many competing demands?
    d. Are time and tools available?
    e. Are there traditions, policies, or ego barriers?
    f. Is the job physically a mess?
12. What are the limits on possible solutions?
    a. Are these solutions that would be considered unacceptable to the organization?
    b. Do key decision-makers have preferred solutions?
    c. Are these solutions beyond the organization's time and money resources?

By following this flowchart of 12 questions, you can analyze nearly any performance problem facing your organization.

Organizational Analysis

The third type of analysis looks at the organization. This look will show the type of information you need to conduct a comprehensive organizational review.

When you begin an organizational analysis, you must make some fundamental decisions about the focus of the study. You can study the entire organization, study a type of managerial function, that is, human resource management, or study a unit or division within the organization. Once you find the focus, you can turn your attention to the evaluation phase of organizational analysis.

You will do the majority of your internal consulting activities during the evaluation phase. You will also conduct personal interviews, design and implement questionnaires to collect data, and observe the performance and behavior of individual employees during this phase.

The "process factor" is the first part of the evaluation phase that includes five separate analyses designed to look at a particular part of the entire organization, a managerial function, or a division within the organization. First, you examine the economic outlook of the organization to determine its present or future condition. This activity is important to predict its financial stability and readiness for change. In other words, a healthy organization, or at least one that has the capacity to be healthy, is more likely to be receptive to new and innovative ideas, systems, and training programs. It will also be in a better position to take advantage of the potential opportunities.

Second, you look at the adequacy of the organizational structure. This examination includes the design of the organization's communications, lines of command, divisions of labor, and span of control. Each of these elements provides insights into how the organization functions and the potential to carry out change.

Third, you examine the adequacy of control, including leadership patterns, the style of the organization, and the formal and informal communication systems within the organization. The relationship between employees and management is important to study to determine their willingness and desire to implement change, and the confidence each has in the other.

Fourth, for a proper evaluation, you must get employees to supply you with their individual perceptions of the organization, observations of employee-manager relationships, information about the operation and structure of the organization, and access to essential records. Therefore, you must protect employees who help you in this step. If you do not, you will not have open and honest disclosure, which will reduce the chance of adequate analysis and interpretation of the organization.

Fifth, you need to find the practices (methods of operation) of the organization. This activity refers to how the organization makes and implements changes, communicates, integrates employees into the organization as well as into the decision-making process, and rewards employees for outstanding service and performance.

"Interpretation" is the second part of the evaluation, and it is the actual analysis of the organization and its problems. During this phase, you decide the method of analysis, conduct the analysis, and interpret the information (data and perceptions collected during the process-factor phase). Then, you can develop recommendations that bring about the change and/or interventions that will improve performance and organizational efficiency.

The last phase of organizational analysis is the presentation of your findings and recommendations for change. This phase may include an informal presentation, a written report, and a formal, final presentation.

To begin, you should give an overview of the evaluation you conducted and how it relates to your recommendations. This

Analysis Checklist

☐ What type of problem is facing your organization?

    ☐ *Performance gap:* Deficiences in the way employees carry out their assignment or duties.

    ☐ *Management gap:* Deficiencies in the way people are managed or motivated in the organization.

    ☐ *Organizational gap:* Deficiencies in the way an organization is conceived and designed.

    ☐ *Type of Intervention*

        ☐ Performance gap = Training and HRD

        ☐ Management gap = Changing management techniques and practices

        ☐ Organizational gap = Organizational development techniques and practices

☐ What is the current situation?

_____

_____

_____

☐ What is the desired situation?

_____

_____

_____

☐ How can you gather information or data to support your problem statement?

    ☐ Focus groups
    ☐ Interviews
    ☐ Questionnaires
    ☐ Observations

☐ Why are these approaches appropriate?

_____

_____

_____

☐ What does the organizational leadership prefer?

_____

_____

_____

information is presented off-the-record so managers, supervisors, and executives can react before findings, recommendations, and interventions become official. It is important to integrate the insights and perceptions of managers, supervisors, and executives as well as to hear their suggestions about the most appropriate approaches, to ensure your recommendations and interventions are adopted by decision-makers.

A written report formally documents the analysis, proposed recommendations, and interventions. It includes the method of analysis, supportive data and information, and the perceptions and opinions of employees. A written report also gives a record of your efforts and activities and is evidence of your performance.

After the written report is completed, you can make a formal presentation to persuade organization decision-makers to adopt your recommendations. You'll need an impressive and convincing presentation, using media that best complements your presentation skills and personality.

Internal consultants must begin to think analytically. You must learn to ask "why" before acting. To do this, it is important to understand the importance and value of the analysis process. You must define problems, determine where interventions can have the most positive effects, gather evidence to support your point of view, appreciate the preferences of organizational leaders, and know how to proceed. You must also be able to conduct task, performance, and organization analyses. Each gives critical information about employee performance and organizational effectiveness.

Chapter Four

The Evolution from Design and Implementation to Performance Management

The two most common processes in HRD are design and implementation. Design includes developing training programs and other interventions by assessing needs, setting learning objectives, designing or selecting a learning activity, implementing training strategies, and evaluating outcomes. This process is also known as *programming*.[1] Programming consists of nine interrelated phases often referred to as the program planning, design, and evaluation process (PPD&E). The nine phases include (see Figure 4–1):

- Phase 1: Philosophy of teaching and learning.
- Phase 2: The needs assessment.
- Phase 3: Feedback.
- Phase 4: Program design.
- Phase 5: Program development.
- Phase 6: Program implementation.
- Phase 7: Program management.
- Phase 8: Evaluation.
- Phase 9: Accountability.

Each phase of the program planning, design, and evaluation process serves as a foundation for the other. The activities conducted by HRD practitioners in each phase are based on this relationship.

While the design and implementation processes are extremely important to producing positive outcomes within HRD, neverthe-

FIGURE 4–1
The Program Planning, Design, and Evaluation Process

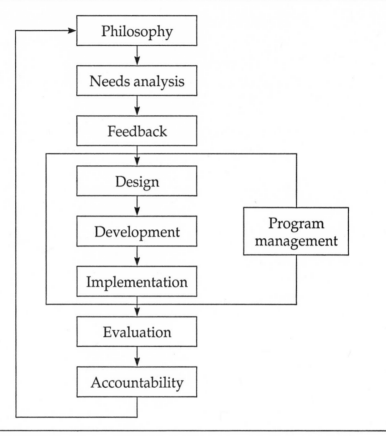

Source: J. W. Gilley and S. A. Eggland, *Principles of Human Development*, © 1989
Addison-Wesley. Publishing Co. Reprinted by permission of Addison-Wesley
Publishing Co., Inc. Reading, MA.

less, they serve only as springboards for internal consultants. They are the foundation that enables internal consultants to become actively involved in performance management. Therefore, it is important for us to discuss briefly each of the nine phases of the program planning, design, and evaluation process to show their importance and relationship to performance management.

DESIGN PROCESS

Phase 1: Philosophy of Teaching and Learning

The first step is to find your philosophical orientation to the teaching and learning process—your personal orientation, training style, or preferred approach to teaching and learning. You can then use this style as a filter for each of the next eight phases of the design process.

Your style or approach will give you a framework for decision-making and selecting materials and methods. This filter should be used as a guide when designing needs assessments, identifying learning objectives and activities, and matching media with activities. In other words, your philosophical orientation to teaching and learning should be used as a reference when you are planning, designing, developing and implementing any program.

Phase 2: Needs Analysis

Needs analysis refers to finding the difference between what is and what should be. The gap between these two is considered the need of the individual, group and organization. In HRD, proficiency (knowledge, skills, attitudes), performance, or organizational situations best describe where these gaps are found. We examined this process in detail in Chapter 3.

Phase 3: Feedback

To make certain that vital decision-makers within the organization have the opportunity to express their points of view before you design a training program or other intervention, it is important to give them an opportunity to provide feedback. You will enable managers and supervisors to express concerns and supply their input into the types of training programs and interventions you design. When they have some "ownership" in the program, they will better support and defend you and the training programs and interventions you design.

This feedback phase of the design process is often overlooked, but it is very critical to the success of HRD. It is also a second validation of the needs assessments you would have conducted previously. This phase can often prevent unnecessary design and development costs, and in many cases, can significantly improve the quality of the training programs and interventions.

Phase 4: Program Design

Once an agreement has been reached about the needs or performance problems of individuals or groups, you can begin designing programs that improve performance and address individual needs. The program design phase is based on the information discovered in the needs analysis phase, which is further analyzed during the feedback phase.

The program design phase is the heart of the design process. Based on the information collected during the needs analysis, internal consultants should: (1) develop learning objectives, (2) develop learning activities, (3) structure the sequence for learning objectives and activities, (4) develop experiential-learning activities, and (5) find instructional media, materials, and methods that are appropriate.

Phase 5: Program Development

Once you have completed the first four phases, you can begin translating design programs into actual training materials and strategies. During this phase, you develop detailed lesson plans, instructional strategies, instructional materials, and learning materials. Each of these is used extensively by trainers and facilitators during the implementation phase.

Phase 6: Program Implementation

The principle architect during the design phase, up to this point, has been the program designer. Implementation, however, is the trainer's and facilitator's primary responsibility.

Trainers and facilitators focus on setting up appropriate learning environments, using the proper methods of instruction, matching and using materials and media with learning activities, identifying the instructional strategies to be used during the training program or intervention, and actually conducting the instructional event. Implementation is, by far, the most visual activity within the entire HRD process and the one where HRD practitioners can gain credibility. Therefore, it is extremely critical that implementation be conducted by highly competent and talented individuals.

We would caution you that implementation (training) is often the most overused and oversubscribed approach to performance improvement. Many training programs cannot be supported as having a direct impact on behavioral change, performance improvement, or improved organizational effectiveness. Implementation is, however, an extremely important phase, one that internal consultants cannot neglect.

Phase 7: Program Management

This phase actually overlaps the last three (design, development, and implementation), because every training program needs a structure by which to sequence, manage, and record instructional events.[2] The principal purpose of program management is to keep accurate information about the learners and their performance. As more and more organizations demand financial accounting for the dollars spent on training programs and other interventions, these records become an increasingly important dimension of the program planning, design, and evaluation process. If done correctly, program management supplies excellent documentation for internal consultants who need to justify the worth, effects, impacts, and efficiency of the program.

Phase 8: Evaluation

There are several reasons why it is necessary to evaluate training programs and interventions. The primary reason is to decide if the training program or intervention carried out the desired objectives. In other words, did the training program or intervention help the participant develop adequate knowledge, skills, and attitudes to close the gap between what is and what should be? Did performance improve and has organizational effectiveness improved?

Another purpose for evaluating training programs and interventions is to find the strengths and weaknesses of each. This activity is done to confirm the design that was used and decide if the program was developed and implemented correctly.

Finally, evaluation helps determine the cost/benefit relationship of each training program or intervention. This check is done to assess the value received by the organization for the expenses allotted. This test is often referred to as the "justification phase" of program evaluation.

In the next chapter, we discuss in detail the importance of the transfer of learning that occurs during this phase. All too often, behaviors improve for a short time after training or an intervention, but they are not reinforced or encouraged by managers, supervisors, and organizational leaders, so they begin to decline. If behaviors are eventually extinguished, the expenses incurred by the organization were wasted.

Phase 9: Accountability

During this phase, you should use the information gathered in the evaluation phase and carry out the necessary changes. All participants in training programs and interventions are responsible for their actions. These participants include the internal consultants, program designers, trainers and facilitators, employees, managers and supervisors, executives, and other organizational leaders.

EVOLVING FROM DESIGN AND IMPLEMENTATION TO PERFORMANCE MANAGEMENT

The program planning, design, and evaluation process gives an overview of various internal consulting activities. The design phase consists of the design and development components within the program planning, design, and evaluation process. The implementation phase of HRD makes up the implementation part of the PPD&E.

The activities which make up the program management, evaluation, and accountability phases of the PPD&E are part of performance management. Another way of showing this is to think of the last six phases of the PPD&E as a stairway. The first three steps: design, development, and implementation, are prerequisites to the final three steps, program management, evaluation, and accountability. Without the first three steps, there would be no foundation for which to complete your path. Since the ultimate goal of moving up the stairway is to reach the top step, it is critical to have a solid foundation.

In the same way, the performance management activities of internal consultants need a solid foundation. Design, development, and implementation are the foundational activities to the more important tasks of performance management. In other words, the outputs of the design, development, and implementation phases of PPD&E are training programs and interventions. These serve as tools for increasing participants' knowledge and skills and improving attitudes, which, ultimately, if applied and used, should improve performance and organizational effectiveness.

The training programs and interventions are, however, the principal responsibilities of instructional designers, trainers, and facilitators. They are not the primary focus of internal consultants. Internal consultants must go beyond training programs and interventions to making certain that performance improvement occurs by using performance management techniques within the organization.

PERFORMANCE MANAGEMENT

During the performance management process, internal consultants' primary responsibility is to train and educate managers and supervisors of their role. How much an HRD practitioner becomes involved in performance management will decide, to a great extent, the role played by the internal consultant. We have included a performance management checklist at the end of this chapter.

Historically, HRD practitioners have been involved in design, development, and implementation of training programs and interventions. They focus their attention on designing and delivering content that improves the skills and knowledge of participants. Therefore, HRD practitioners are indirectly involved in the performance improvement process because learning transfer is primarily the responsibility of the participants.

In contrast, performance management requires the active involvement of a change agent using positive reinforcement and feedback to improve performance. This activity is a direct, rather than indirect, approach to performance improvement. The change agent in this situation is the internal consultant.

Performance improvement is a systematic, *data-oriented* approach to managing employees.[3] This approach uses positive reinforcement and feedback to maximize performance. To decide if a performance management procedure is effective, you must identify the behavior and the results to be affected. This activity is best done by establishing current behaviors (baseline) using a variety of measurement techniques. This baseline allows you to test the effectiveness of motivational strategies used to improve learning transfer and reinforcement of new behaviors.

Internal consultants are responsible for fostering an environment for performance management. Managers and supervisors have the primary responsibility of providing motivational strategies that ultimately bring about a change in employees' behavior. To change performance, you must first change what people do.

A combination of behaviors is referred to as *performance*. This may include a single activity or a series of activities directed at an outcome or goal. Regardless, performance is a complex and difficult process to observe and effect. For you to assist managers and supervisors in improving performance, you must focus your attention on behavior. In other words, direct your attention to the ''parts'' of performance rather than the whole. This attention helps employees change their performance *one behavior at a time*. Each behavior can be reinforced, and consequences can be received for demonstrating behaviors that can improve performance.

In the mid-1950s, Albert Ellis identified a process whereby performance can be changed by focusing on two events. They include what comes *before* a behavior and what comes *after* it. He refers to this model as the *ABC model* of behavior change. He believes when you are trying to influence behavior before it occurs, you are using *antecedents*. On the other hand, when you are attempting to influence behavior by doing something after it occurs, you are focusing on the *consequences*. Performance management must include antecedents and consequences to improve employee performance.

Antecedents

An antecedent is a person, place, thing, or event coming before a behavior that encourages an employee to perform that behavior.[4] This event can include any stimulus that causes an employee to take an action. For example, a ringing telephone prompts an employee to pick it up and answer it. This example illustrates that a stimulus (a ringing phone) elicits a response (picking up the phone).

The behavior of other people is also classified as an antecedent. This concept is often referred to as *modeling*. For example, a salesperson who demonstrates proper interviewing techniques when deciding the needs and wants of a client is practicing modeling behavior. The actions of managers and supervisors also influence the behavior of employees. If these actions and words give mixed messages, you can see why the phrase "do as I say, not as I do" can confuse and negatively impact behavior.

For managers and supervisors to choose the right antecedents, they must understand the relationship of antecedents to that consequence. Any antecedent that can be directly linked to a consequence can better effect desired performance of employees. Antecedents that clearly describe expectations or desired performance, such as job descriptions or performance standards, stand a better chance of affecting behavior than ones that are not specifically clear.

Antecedents that have a history of being associated with a specific consequence are also ones that can dramatically affect the performance of employees. For example, arriving to work late can result in suspensions or dismissal of employees or dramatically impact or affect the tardiness of employees. Another type of antecedent that has a greater propensity for improving performance are behaviors that occur just before the desired performance. For example, writing a comprehensive outline before writing a letter is an example of this type of an antecedent.

Internal consultants can help managers and supervisors improve performance by using common types of antecedents:[5]

- Providing job aids (instructions, directions, flowcharts, checklist).
- Training (films, books, tapes).
- Supplying tools and materials.

- Providing policies and procedures.
- Arranging the work environment (i.e., temperature, lighting, noise level).
- Holding meetings.

Consequences

Consequences are activities that follow behavior and they change the chance that the behavior will reoccur in the future. Consequences occur naturally and are different from punishment.[6] Punishment is a deliberate act to inflict predetermined outcomes that alter or affect a person's behavior. People doing a behavior are the ones responsible for that behavior and, therefore, will receive the naturally occurring results.

In an organizational setting, managers and supervisors can arrange natural consequences that occur after a behavior. The result is that a behavior is not designed to inflict punitive action, but to focus on motivating and improving behavior. Therefore, punishment is a negative outcome inflicted on employees by managers and supervisors, while consequences are naturally occurring results of employees' behavior.

Managers and supervisors must understand that people do not perform correctly on the job for many reasons. First, they don't know what to do. In other words, the job responsibilities or job description has not been fully communicated to them. Therefore, employees either fail to perform the behaviors in the correct sequence or they drop critical or specific behaviors.

Second, employees don't know how to do the job. This situation is often the result of inadequate training and development activities that are the responsibility of managers and supervisors.

Third, there are barriers in the work environment that either prevent or discourage the performance of specific tasks. Again, the responsibility of identifying and eliminating such barriers falls on the managers and supervisors.

Finally, employees don't do what managers and supervisors desire because employees simply don't want to.

The first three reasons are a direct result of inadequate understanding of antecedents. Lack of a job description, lack of proper training, and barriers and obstacles to performance are all things that come before a behavior.

The last reason, however, is a result of inappropriate consequences. In other words, people do what they do because the consequence supports it. Thus, employees who don't do a job simply because they don't want to are ones who aren't receiving a direct consequence for their actions. This concept is often referred to as *reinforcement.*

Reinforcement.   Reinforcements can be used to affect behavior in one of two ways: they can either increase or decrease it. Managers and supervisors can use positive and negative reinforcements. Behavior will increase when employees get something they want or avoid something they don't want. Behavior can decrease when employees get something they don't want or managers and supervisors withhold or take away something employees want.

For managers and supervisors to receive what they want, they must provide positive reinforcers. These are any consequence that increase the chance that the behavior that precedes it will occur more often.[7] For example, in a training class, an instructor could say "that's an excellent idea, thank you for your comment" to a participant for volunteering an answer or critical information. This type of praise gives encouragement to class participants to become involved in a discussion of key concepts. This type of reinforcer will improve the chance that the behavior (class participation) will occur more often.

For employees to avoid something they don't want, managers and supervisors should use negative reinforcers. Negative reinforcers are consequences that people work hard to avoid, for example, receiving a failing grade in school. Receiving negative feedback about performance after completing a task is an example of this type of reinforcer. It encourages employees to avoid something they don't want, which results in a change in their behavior.

All too often, managers and supervisors use this type of coercive technique to impact the behavior of their employees. Internal consultants should help managers and supervisors understand that focusing only on negative reinforcers will result in demoralized, manipulated, and discouraged employees.

When employees get something they don't want, it is referred to as *punishment*. It is often predetermined and prescribed as a result of certain activities. Therefore, a punisher is anything that happens to an employee that decreases behavior. The example used before, getting suspended or fired for coming to work late, is an example of a punishment.

In many situations, employees fail to get something they want. If this type of reinforcement occurs, it is referred to as *extinction*. Extinction means withholding or nondelivery of reinforcements for previously reinforced behavior. In other words, behavior will tend to be extinguished if previously reinforced behavior is no longer reinforced.

An example of extinction would be an employee who had received continuous salary increases for his performance. One year, however, he does not receive a salary increase. It is highly likely that his performance over the next few months will be dramatically affected because he did not receive the reward (reinforcer) he wanted or *expected*.

Managers and supervisors may try to soften or affect the decrease in performance by explaining why a salary increase was not given, but these explanations can easily be rationalized by the employee. Therefore, the result may well be that the employee begins to perform at a less than acceptable level.

POSITIVE REINFORCEMENT: THE PREFERRED CONSEQUENCE

While all reinforcement techniques have their uses, positive reinforcement is the most effective in helping people achieve improved work performance. Negative reinforcement only produces a level of performance necessary to escape or avoid punishment. Managers and supervisors may use punishment and extinction to change behavior but these methods tend to weaken behavior, rather than strengthen it.

The goal of an organization is not to weaken performance, but to improve it. Therefore, punishment and extinction serve as demotivators rather than motivators for most employees. Managers and supervisors should avoid them whenever possible.

Positive reinforcement has many positive side effects. First, it can help improve and foster good supervisor/employee relationships. It can increase and improve morale of employees and their attitudes toward the organization. Positive reinforcement helps create a climate of positive outcomes and accountabilities. Finally, positive reinforcement is needed because people need this type of feedback.

DELIVERING POSITIVE REINFORCEMENT

For positive reinforcement to be accepted by employees, it should reflect the personality and style of the manager or supervisor. Employees are very skeptical of a manager or supervisor who "becomes a different person" when giving positive reinforcement. It is very important that the employee believe the feedback being given.

Internal consultants must teach managers and supervisors to give reinforcements immediately after the desired behavior. This promptness enables employees to link their behavior to the reinforcement. Delaying positive reinforcement will often confuse employees. Unless feedback is delivered promptly (immediately after performance), employees may attribute the reinforcer to a behavior that the manager or supervisor is not attempting to reinforce, therefore, accidentally reinforcing the wrong behavior.

In addition, delayed reinforcement can increase the risk that intermediate behaviors between the desired behavior and the delayed reinforcer may get reinforced. This result may require further communication by the manager or supervisor, which can add to an employee's misunderstanding of the desired behavior.

Reinforcements should also be specific, which means telling people exactly what they did that you liked. Being specific is very important early in the acquisition of a new skill or knowledge because employees need the greatest amount of reinforcement at this time. It is not enough to tell an employee of a job well done, but rather, exactly *what* was done to call for the positive reinforcement.

Internal consultants must convince managers and supervisors that giving positive reinforcement must first and foremost be a sincere effort, which includes *what* a manager or supervisor says and *how* they say it. If the reinforcer is not sincere, it is not likely to reinforce the desired behavior. Managers and supervisors should be taught never to tell a person something they don't mean. If employees are not performing the behavior correctly, they should not be told they are. This will further confuse employees when it's time to correct the behavior or when a punishment results because they didn't do it correctly. Employees will resent managers or supervisors for their lack of sincerity and honesty.

Sincerity also helps employees to be receptive to negative reinforcers, punishments, or extinction activities. Employees tend to work best for managers and supervisors whom they respect.

Sincerity is difficult to convey because it is hard to communicate to every employee exactly the same kind of positive reinforcement. Employees quickly catch on to the lack of sincerity of such phrases as "have a nice day," "you're doing a good job," or "we appreciate you." They recognize that unearned compliments, flattery, or insincere comments do not motivate them to perform their jobs better.

Finally, humor and sarcasm should never be used as a form of reinforcement. They are very hard to communicate effectively and are often misunderstood by employees.

The more frequently an employee is reinforced for a desired performance, the stronger the performance will be.[8] Therefore, it is important that employees receive reinforcements continuously. The question is always, "how much is enough?" The answer to this question involves several factors that only the situation can dictate. One of the best ways to decide the proper frequency of reinforcement is to develop a "reinforcement log," which allows you to track reinforcements and subsequent performance. This data will allow managers and supervisors to know what the effects of reinforcers were in improving performance.

Finally, reinforcers should be given in a clear and concise manner. Many managers and supervisors use a technique where they begin with a positive reinforcement, give negative reinforcement, and then give additional positive reinforcement. This method is known as the *sandwich approach*. By providing a negative that is sandwiched between two positives, employees generally only focus on the information presented in the middle of the interaction. They rarely focus on the two positives given at the beginning and the end.

In addition, employees recognize this approach of managers and supervisors and don't listen to the initial reinforcer because they are aware that a negative reinforcer is to follow. Further, the reinforcer given last is often not heard because the employee is focusing on the negative reinforcer previously given.

Another reason the sandwich method fails to improve performance is that it is not directly focused on a specific behavior. Internal consultants should help managers and supervisors link reinforcers to *each behavior* they are trying to change. If a negative reinforcer is appropriate, it should be presented independent of other reinforcers.

MEASUREMENT

Internal consultants have a responsibility to help managers and supervisors analyze performance. Once they have identified a performance, managers and supervisors can begin to diagnose the performance, find the cause and specify or prescribe any necessary treatment. This concept is often referred to as *measurement*.

Measurement is used in performance management to increase the proper delivery of reinforcement. Measurement allows managers and supervisors to show small changes in performance that otherwise could not be seen through casual observation. Also, measurement helps managers and supervisors figure out why employees do not do what is expected of them—is it that employees don't know what to do? don't know how to do it? have barriers that prevent performance? or simply don't want to perform? In this way, managers can decide whether the lack of performance is caused by an antecedent or by not finding the consequences resulting from performance.

PERFORMANCE FEEDBACK

Performance feedback is information about performance that helps an individual change the performance. The term *feedback* includes all four types of reinforcement, both positive and negative. It also includes other information that should be shared with employees to help them improve their performance, such as job descriptions, performance standards, and skills audit.

Many times, the term *feedback* is used interchangeably for information and data. Information and data, however, do not tell an employee which behavior to change or how. Many managers and supervisors supply a lot of information and data but very little feedback.

The Value of Feedback

Feedback is important because it is essential to learning. It helps employees know when they are performing their jobs correctly. This knowledge is the first step to improving quality, performance, and organizational effectiveness.

Feedback is often the least expensive and easiest method managers and supervisors can use to start improving performance; however, managers do not provide adequate feedback mainly because they tried it, and it didn't work. Many managers and supervisors, however, cannot differentiate between feedback and information and data. Also, they don't understand that feedback alone may not improve performance. Appropriate rewards and compensation are also necessary to motivate employees to improve their performance.

Research has shown that feedback alone produces the lowest level of consistent effects in changing performance.[9] Feedback, consequences (rewards), and goal setting, however, together produce the most positive and consistent effects in changing performance.

Characteristics of Effective Feedback

Feedback appears to be a very simple concept; however, there are some characteristics that tend to increase or decrease its effectiveness. As an internal consultant, you need to help managers and supervisors understand each of these characteristics. They include:

- Give specific how-to information.
- Give feedback on a performance the person can control.

Performance Management

> ☐ Why don't employees perform their jobs correctly?
>
> | **Situation** | **Action** |
> |---|---|
> | ☐ They don't know what to do. ——————→ | **Job Descriptions** |
> | ☐ They don't know how to do the ——————→ job. | **Training** |
> | ☐ There are barriers in the work—————→ environment which either prevent or discourage the performance of their jobs. | **Removal of Barriers** |
> | ☐ They don't do their jobs because ——→ they don't want to. | **Performance Management** |

Measurement Techniques

☐ What measurement techniques can you use to determine current behavior?
  - ☐ Observations
  - ☐ Records and Reports
  - ☐ Work Sample
  - ☐ Performance Standards

☐ Why are these techniques appropriate?

_____

_____

_____

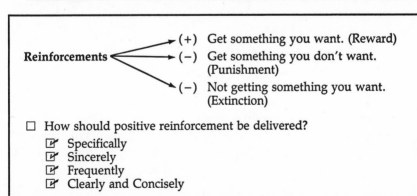

> **Reinforcements**
> - (+) Get something you want. (Reward)
> - (−) Get something you don't want. (Punishment)
> - (−) Not getting something you want. (Extinction)
>
> ☐ How should positive reinforcement be delivered?
>   - ☑ Specifically
>   - ☑ Sincerely
>   - ☑ Frequently
>   - ☑ Clearly and Concisely

Characteristics of Effective Feedback

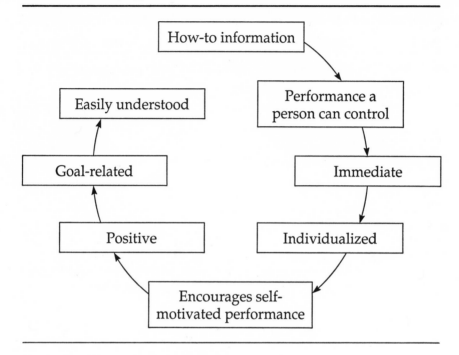

- Give immediate feedback.
- Give individualized feedback.
- Encourage self-monitored performance.
- Give feedback by the person in charge, if not self-monitored.
- Give positive feedback.
- Give goal-related feedback.
- Give easily understood feedback.[10]

Each of these characteristics can improve feedback that managers and supervisors give to employees.

You should monitor and measure whether or not managers and supervisors are performing this role correctly. In this way, you are directly improving performance and organizational effectiveness.

Chapter Five

Improving the Transfer of Learning: The Internal Consultant's Primary Dilemma

At a regional professional development meeting of William M. Mercer, Incorporated, Robert Lindgren, regional vice president, expressed his belief that professional development activities and training are of little value if senior members in an organization don't support the knowledge and skills taught during training. Applying new skills to the day-to-day job, or "learning transfer," is not only the responsibility of the employees who took part in training, but also of managers, supervisors, and the organization.

John Kotter of Harvard University said that the lack of involvement by top management was, in his opinion, the principal reason why learning was not transferred to the job. The American Society for Training and Development has reported that over $200 billion is spent each year by corporations for training and development activities. But at the same time, more and more organizations and top executives are questioning that investment in light of the returns received. Therefore, as internal consultants, we are faced with an ever-increasing tension between spending dollars and improving training performance and organizational effectiveness. The lack of return on investment realized by providing training sums up the severity of the learning transfer problem.

Robert Brinkerhoff, professor, Western Michigan University, believes that the learning transfer problem can be traced back to the very method by which internal consultants and HRD practitioners approach their job responsibilities. In thinking about the four phases used in HRD, analysis, implementation, transfer, and evaluation, he reminds us that HRD practitioners tend to focus on the implementation phase. This is the phase we understand best, the phase we've spent the majority of our time researching and the phase that requires the majority of an HRD practitioner's time.

Brinkerhoff believes that if internal consultants would spend an equal amount of time on analysis, transfer, and evaluation, we would be more likely to achieve the desired outcomes. We know a fair amount about analysis and a great deal about evaluation. But most internal consultants do not conduct either process correctly. This failure inhibits learning transfer.

Another inhibitor is that internal consultants, managers, supervisors, and employees do not meet their responsibilities during the transfer phase. The employees have the responsibility to apply and transfer the skills and knowledge gained during training. Managers and supervisors have the responsibility to remove barriers that prohibit transfer and to support learning. Internal consultants are responsible for providing an environment that encourages employees to transfer skills and knowledge and encourages managers and supervisors to remove barriers and supply supportive activities.

Brinkerhoff challenges internal consultants to focus attention on the transfer phase, while keeping in mind the importance of analysis, implementation, and evaluation. He also challenges researchers of HRD to supply evidence that will improve our understanding of the transfer phase.

NINE ADDITIONAL BARRIERS

There are other reasons why learning transfer does not occur on the job. For example:

1. Lack of reinforcement on the job.
2. Interference with immediate (work) environment.
3. Nonsupport of organizational culture.
4. Trainee's perception of impractical training programs.
5. Trainee's perception of irrelevant training content.
6. Trainee's discomfort with change and associated effort.

7. Separation from inspirational support of the trainer.

8. Trainee's perception of poorly designed and delivered training.

9. Pressure from peers to resist changes.

The first three barriers can be most influenced by management and organizational leaders. The next five can be best addressed by internal consultants responsible for providing training and design. The last barrier can be best addressed by employees themselves as they look at their personal motives about learning transfer.

The first three barriers (lack of reinforcement, interference, non-support of organizational culture) are ones produced and fostered by managers, supervisors, and the organization. It is the internal consultant's responsibility, however, to communicate to this group that the organization has invested a great deal of time, energy, effort, and money by allowing them to participate in training and other interventions. By pointing out this expense, you will have made managers and supervisors more aware of the importance of training and interventions.

The investment is best spent if managers and supervisors become active participants with employees before, during and after training has occurred. This participation includes reinforcing the skills and knowledge acquired during training, cutting excessive workloads during periods when new skills and knowledge are being developed, and providing a supportive work environment that is conducive to learning transfer. Internal consultants should use evaluation techniques such as cost/benefit analysis and result evaluations to prove that training and interventions, indeed, have a positive impact on the organization.

Internal consultants can best impact barriers four to eight by designing, developing, and delivering training programs and interventions that are practical, problem-focused, and realistic. You should be certain that such programs and interventions are properly designed and provide for employee involvement during learning. Also, you should make yourself available to participants in training programs and interventions shortly after such activities so you can reinforce, encourage, motivate, and persuade participants to use the skills and knowledge taught.

Last, be realistic in your quest for learning transfer. Recognize that employees are often uncomfortable with new skills and knowledge because it interferes with present skills and knowledge. This uncomfortable state causes resistance to the new skill or knowledge, especially if the new skill or knowledge makes the employees feel inadequate or awkward. Therefore, you must take into account this type of proactive learning interference within the individual. Using job or performance aids that reinforce the skills or knowledge, taught in a user-friendly and supportive manner, are excellent tools that help employees overcome proactive interference.

The last barrier (number 9) refers to the pressure by peers to resist change. While on the surface this barrier may appear to be an individual struggle, it is really the responsibility of managers and supervisors to provide an environment where other employees do not discourage the acquisition of new skills and knowledge. This goal can best be carried out by communicating to all employees the value and importance of training programs and/or interventions and the serious nature by which the organization is addressing such learning and skill deficiencies.

Ways of doing this include asking nonparticipants to help support the organization's learning goals and objectives. Also, keep in mind that people tend to want to please their peers. You can become an active participant in this process by understanding the internal struggle. Talk about it shortly after the end of the training program or intervention or during follow-up interviews and group discussions with participants.

In many cases, internal consultants are as much to blame for the failure of learning transfer as are the managers, supervisors, and the organization. If you have the attitude that it is the learner's responsibility to learn and only your responsibility to provide the new skills and knowledge, you are fostering an environment where learning transfer will fail.

Supplying training and interventions is only one small part of transferring the skills and knowledge to the job. Internal consultants must become agents in the pursuit of learning transfer. You must become proactive and anticipate the barriers previously discussed. You must become active in persuading managers and supervisors of their responsibilities about learning transfer and continue to design and develop training programs and interventions that meet the needs of your client group.

HOW TO FOSTER LEARNING TRANSFER

In 1951, Kurt Lewin provided a classic model in change intervention. He believed that behavior could be best managed by providing a three-step process: unfreezing, change and freezing.

Unfreezing

Change can best occur when managers and supervisors supply an environment that is conducive for employees to examine their own work performance. This activity is done to show areas of strengths and weaknesses and to incorporate new approaches to the job. This activity is called the *unfreezing* phase. During this period, employees look at their attitudes, beliefs, and values that combine to produce their behaviors. If behavior is to change, the attitudes, beliefs, and values of employees must also change. Lewin believed that if employees are encouraged to examine their present performance, determine strengths and weaknesses, and take part in learning, they will be willing to incorporate new behaviors.

It is your responsibility, therefore, to be an active participant with employees and management during this unfreezing phase. You must make certain that the skills and knowledge given are consistent with, and not contrary to, the existing skills and knowledge of employees. In other words, there must be a slow and deliberate approach to changing behavior. A radical approach will often be perceived by employees as a threat and will severely hamper the acquisition of new behaviors.

Change

Lewin believed that every individual is in a constant search for equilibrium. Equilibrium is a steady state, balanced between the opposing forces that drive behavior toward change and those that restrain it. Change is often resisted because it disrupts an individual's equilibrium. Therefore, internal consultants must introduce change in ways that reduce resistance. You must drop barriers to change by introducing change to individuals in a context they understand. Let's look at each of these separately.

Individual barriers to transfer are often difficult, if not impossible, to identify. Therefore, it's important that you talk to participants of training programs and interventions to isolate individual barriers. Then, you can help managers and supervisors remove or diminish the barriers that prevent transfer.

Internal consultants can best improve learning transfer by introducing change in such a way that employees are willing to incorporate changes in behavior; for example, by introducing changes in behavior in small portions and considering the world of the learner. Use examples that show your understanding of their world. Develop learning activities and exercises that reflect the participants' context. Use reinforcement and supportive activities after training to show your understanding of the practical realities of the participants' world. Remember, change must be introduced in small, manageable units to be accepted by the participant.

Refreezing

Lewin believes that once change has been introduced and incorporated by participants, they are responsible for *refreezing* the new set of behaviors so they become automatic. To help participants do this, provide reinforcement and follow-up activities after training. Encourage managers and supervisors to foster and encourage future behavioral change by developing reward systems that recognize new behaviors. While it is the participants' responsibility to refreeze behavior, it is your responsibility to create an environment that will help them do so.

Using the Lewin model as background, we would like to provide several strategies for improving the transfer of learning: (1) preparing for change before training, (2) training: an opportunity for involvement and self-reflection, and (3) applications and follow-up strategies after training has occurred.

PREPARING FOR CHANGE

There are several important strategies that can be used to prepare for change. They include:

1. Orient managers and supervisors to their role.

Examples:
Pecos River Learning Center

This is an outward-bound, experimental learning center east of Santa Fe, New Mexico. It was founded by Larry Wilson, former founder and CEO of the Wilson Learning Corporation. The principal activity of Pecos River Learning Center is to conduct outward-bound activities designed to improve teamwork and help senior executives and managers confront their fears and overcome obstacles and barriers.

The center established a process consulting unit in the fall of 1991 to improve learning transfer. The purpose of this unit is to help participants integrate and carry out what they have learned during the outward-bound experience. A process consultant works closely with the executives and managers (who attended the original program), developing implementation strategies, duplicating the training experience with others in the organization, and maintaining proper and effective communication among participants.

Philosophically, the leadership at Pecos River Learning Center understands that the skills, awareness, and knowledge acquired during training is of little importance unless they are integrated and transferred to the job. The process consulting effort helps ensure that this transfer occurs.

William M. Mercer, Incorporated

The Professional Development Committee of the central region was concerned about the transfer of learning with their project management efforts. They designed a reinforcement strategy using senior consultants teamed with new project managers. Senior consultants attended a modified version of the training program, which helped them understand the concepts and skills taught and how they could provide appropriate feedback to their partners. The new project managers participated in the training program and were required to apply the concepts and skills taught.

Three weeks after the training program, the senior consultants and new project managers met to discuss their progress. They also discussed the barriers that prevented learning transfer and how senior consultants could help remove them. They set up a schedule for follow-up interventions and a method of giving and receiving feedback. Finally, they discussed successes they had experienced since training and experiences that reflected the difficulties they

---

Examples (Continued)

were having applying the concepts and skills. Such modeling partnership can greatly enhance learning transfer, while improving communication and interpersonal interactions.

Walt Disney, Inc.

Disney World has a policy that requires all new employees to participate in an orientation program. While this idea is not unique, it is the way they schedule the program that is different from many other organizations. These orientation programs include senior managers, executives, park maintenance staff, concession workers, and gift shop employees. The program fosters an environment of teamwork and reduces the barriers among differing levels of employees. This effort indirectly provides opportunities that encourage open and honest communication and feedback, the ingredients necessary for learning transfer to occur.

Birkman and Associates

The management consulting firm of Birkman and Associates is headquartered in Houston, Texas. The company provides a personality instrument designed to give insight into one's management style, personality characteristics, and reactions under stress and needs. It supplies training and support to over 1,000 independent management consultants certified to use its personality instrument.

In an attempt to improve learning transfer, the company maintains a staff that provides immediate interpretation of instrument results, applications, and insights. The company helps independent consultants design management change strategies for organizations it works with. It also provides continuous training support and advanced training for its independent consultants.

---

2. Solicit employees', managers', and supervisors' input before developing training programs and interventions.
3. Develop coaching skills for managers and supervisors.
4. Use cohort work teams during training programs and interventions.
5. Provide alternative training options.

6. Provide training immediately before application.
7. Identify and communicate performance standards.
8. Communicate the importance of training to participants.
9. Communicate management's support for training.
10. Identify rewards that result from adopting new skills and knowledge.

First, internal consultants are responsible for orienting managers and supervisors about their role in the change process. This strategy includes identifying their responsibilities as well as suggesting possible actions they can take part in before change is introduced. In return, managers and supervisors must accept their responsibilities proactively and become involved in the change process.

Second, you can greatly improve the possibilities of change by asking for managers', supervisors', and employees' input before designing and developing training programs and interventions. Asking can be done in a formal or informal manner. In a formal manner, managers, supervisors, and employees can be placed on professional development committees responsible for giving information to internal consultants before they engage in design activities. In an informal manner, you can ask for ideas and suggestions from managers and employees during informal interviews and discussions. Regardless of how you gather it, this information is critical to designing and developing training programs and interventions that are practical, realistic, and problem-centered.

Third, you should help managers and supervisors develop coaching skills to encourage employees to change behaviors. These skills include better listening and communication strategies and feedback techniques. Largely, the development of coaching skills is, in itself, a form of change for many managers and supervisors. When this is the case, use other managers and supervisors for insights and suggestions before training.

Fourth, allow "cohort work teams" to participate in change activities together. These teams include project management, production, and service teams. By allowing an entire work team to take part in a change activity together, it is able to develop a common understanding, language, and context in which change will occur. This, in an indirect way, gives better support and integration of change for team members. This strategy will also help foster and improve the training activity because you can address common questions and concerns in a consistent manner. Cohort work teams end the peer pressure of not changing, brought about by people who do not take part in training programs and interventions.

Fifth, internal consultants can also help employees prepare for change by providing individuals with training options rather than by requiring all individuals to take part in a formal training program. This strategy may appear to be in contrast with the previous one; however, certain individuals may need training options that consider their unique situation and learning style. By having the flexibility to be diverse, you have shown your willingness to treat participants as *individuals*. This action will greatly enhance participants' willingness to engage in self-reflective activities. In addition, training options consider a variety of learning styles that adults possess, which will reinforce the acquisition of new skills and knowledge.

Sixth, giving training and/or interventions that are timely is critical to accepting change. When new skills or knowledge can't be applied right away, learning transfer can fail. However, training that is prompt, providing new skills and knowledge immediately before it is applied, greatly enhances transfer. Adults learn best when training is problem-focused and when they're facing situations or circumstances that test their present state. This idea is consistent with Lewin's concept of unfreezing.

Seventh, you should help managers and supervisors identify and communicate the performance standards in which their employees are to be judged. Such standards serve as the minimum requirements for excellence. They can include skills, knowledge, or attitudes desired by managers and supervisors. Performance standards provide an atmosphere for employees to look at their current skills and knowledge vis-à-vis the job to be done. This analysis could well be the most critical activity employees take part in as they prepare for change. Without this information, employees can't measure their performance against performance desired by the organization.

Eighth, internal consultants should also encourage managers and supervisors to communicate the importance of the training to their employees. This strategy will help employees appreciate the time, energy, and effort they are exchanging for new skills and knowledge. It also helps employees answer the question, "What's in it for me?"

Ninth, you should help managers and supervisors communicate their support for training. It is not enough to simply communicate the importance of new skills and knowledge; it is equally important for managers and supervisors to communicate their willingness to support a participant's application of new skills and knowledge on the job. This requires managers and supervisors to be patient as employees try to acquire new skills and knowledge, particularly if performance dips as employees struggle to integrate new skills and knowledge. Patience by managerial supervisors will help foster a more supportive work environment and encourage employees to take some risks in improving work processes and procedures.

Tenth, you should encourage managers and supervisors to find rewards and give recognition for acquiring new skills and knowledge. These should be announced before employees participate in training and interventions. Employees need to be aware of such rewards and recognitions as an incentive to participate in change.

Each of these 10 strategies will prepare employees to take part in training activities and interventions that will help them consider behaviors other than the ones they are now using. Proper preparation before the change will allow successful unfreezing of current behaviors.

TRAINING: OPPORTUNITIES FOR INVOLVEMENT AND SELF-REFLECTION

Internal consultants have an opportunity to embrace a multitude of strategies during the training process to foster and improve learning transfer. Each of these strategies can greatly enhance the learning that occurs during the training event, and provide opportunities for ever-increasing learning transfer:

1. Provide a positive learning environment.
2. Encourage learner participation.
3. Provide practical and work-related learning experiences.
4. Develop application-oriented learning objectives.

5. Develop employees' readiness to learn.
6. Answer the question for participants, ''What's in it for me?''
7. Provide individual feedback.
8. Develop job-performance training aids.
9. Develop strategies for applying new skills and knowledge.
10. Help managers and supervisors understand the importance of minimal interruptions during training.
11. Encourage managers and supervisors to transfer employees' workloads during training.
12. Give rewards and recognition to employees after training.
13. Create support groups back on the job.
14. Develop personal performance contracts to be used to monitor change.

On occasion, internal consultants are asked to lead training programs and facilitate other interventions. When this occurs, you have an excellent opportunity to increase and impact learning transfer. You must first provide an environment that is conducive to learning by being receptive to divergent ideas and thoughts. You must also be patient with individuals who have difficulty mastering basic skills and knowledge. You can encourage interaction among participants by supplying activities that allow participants to work in small groups.

In addition, practical and work-related learning activities encourage participation and interaction of participants. These activities should be applications-oriented and determined by the type of learning objectives of the training program or intervention. These activities greatly help participants apply new skills and integrate new knowledge, which helps end proactive interference (conflict between new skills and knowledge with presently held ones).

Internal consultants should develop learning activities and materials that help participants prepare for training programs. These tools can include articles, books, and newsletters about the topic to be discussed, or self-diagnostic instruments and personality instruments that give the participants some insight about their capabilities, personality, or behavior. The latter tools heighten participants' curiosity and interest. Finally, case studies and discussion games can prepare participants for the topic to be discussed. All of these tools help improve participants' readiness to learn.

At the beginning of every training program or intervention, internal consultants must always discuss the question, "What's in it for me?" This dilemma is the overriding concern of all participants. An excellent way of doing this is to allow participants to express their expectations of the program or intervention as they introduce themselves. You then capture these remarks on paper for the entire group and comment on how the program or intervention will accomplish these expectations or how it can be adjusted to meet them. The paper should then be posted in a central location in the learning environment, so you and the participants can constantly refer back to the needs of the group.

As the program or intervention unfolds, internal consultants can refer to the posted list of expectations and check them off as they are discussed. If the program or intervention lasts longer than one day, the morning review should include how the activities previously engaged in have addressed some of the participants' expectations. Finally, internal consultants should always go over the list of expectations in their last review or conclusion.

You must always give feedback to participants about how well they learned the new skill. Feedback can be both positive and negative. Positive feedback helps improve participants' confidence and keep their self-esteem. It also helps you build a positive relationship with participants during the training program or intervention, which helps later, because internal consultants should be engaged in follow-up and support activities when the program or intervention is over.

Negative feedback can be used, but it should be limited. It is best when internal consultants are trying to help participants extinguish a behavior or attitude that is interfering with a new skill or knowledge. However, negative feedback should never be perceived as overly critical of the person or their point of view. Sarcasm should never be used as a feedback technique. (See Chapter 4 for additional information on feedback.)

Internal consultants have an excellent opportunity to improve learning transfer by designing and developing job-performance training aids that help participants master a skill or integrate knowledge on the job. The job-performance training aid should include all of the necessary steps needed to perform a new skill, sequenced in proper order. In addition, job-performance training aids should include the essential elements of a new policy, procedure, or regulation that employees must integrate. For employees to use job-performance aids correctly, internal consultants should provide time during a training program or intervention to discuss them and give instructions on how they can be used. This instruction will improve their correct application and encourage participants to use the aids on the job.

You can help participants apply new skills and integrate new knowledge by developing strategies for their job applications. This help can be given during training through the use of case studies, discussion games, role-playing, and small-group discussions. Also, internal consultants can help participants apply new skills and knowledge by asking them how they can be used on the job. This open-ended discussion requires participants to reflect on their job duties and responsibilities to determine application, and it becomes the "point of entry" for new skills and knowledge. It is hoped that this knowledge will take seed and begin to flourish.

Internal consultants can also help participants apply new skills by helping participants create work performance contracts and daily logs. Work performance contracts let participants make a commitment to applying and integrating new skills or knowledge. These contracts should include job-related work objectives, methods of application and integration, measurement criteria, and alternative plans. They should be written in a way that encourages participants to apply or integrate a new skill or knowledge rather than in a way that punishes them for not doing so. There should also be a time frame for the application or integration. This schedule could include a final date or a breakdown of several milestone dates to help encourage progress.

Daily logs help participants in two ways. First, they help them to identify the circumstance, events, conditions, and results of each application. This knowledge provides them with a schedule of progress and detailed information that helps explain why it was easy or difficult to apply new skills or knowledge. Second, daily logs serve as a constant reminder that a new skill or knowledge must be practiced or understood. Logs represent a stimulus that encourages participants to apply and integrate new skills or knowledge. You will find the daily log to be a wealth of information as you develop strategies for learning transfer.

It is important to convince managers and supervisors that interruptions during training programs or interventions greatly diminish their effectiveness. Managers and supervisors must understand that an interruption during training suggests that the training is of less importance than the interruption. If change is to occur, employees must be convinced that their participation in training is equal to or greater in importance than any other activity. Therefore, managers and supervisors must keep interruptions to a minimum.

In addition, managers and supervisors should be convinced that transferring the workload during training is critical to applying the new skill and behavior. Employees who take part in training can be quickly demoralized if they arrive back in the workplace and discover two to three days of work to catch up on, while attempting to apply new skills and knowledge. Such overloads become barriers to the integration of these new skills and knowledge. If the workload can be spread out among employees who are not attending the training program, the attitude of participants is greatly enhanced.

You should encourage managers and supervisors to reward and recognize employees after a training program or intervention. While this activity seems to be fairly minor, such ceremonies will communicate to employees the value of training as well as the willingness of managers and supervisors to support skill and knowledge transfer.

Internal consultants should develop support groups of participants in the training program or intervention and important managers and supervisors. Support groups encourage participants to incorporate and apply the new skills and knowledge. Support groups should also have the responsibility of monitoring the acquisition of new skills and knowledge in the workplace. Monitoring should not be done in a manipulative or coercive manner, but in a way that fosters the application of the training provided. In this way, peer groups are positively reinforcing the use of new skills and knowledge rather than encouraging its extinction.

It is your job to serve as the bridge between managers and supervisors, and employees, to create personal performance contracts. Contracts of this type allow management and employees to discuss the goals and objectives desired and create a plan that will help employees improve performance. Performance contracts will help employees receive rewards and recognition. Contracts should be specifically written, quantitatively designed, and established around a time limit. They should be used as a part of the performance appraisal process and incorporated as a benchmark for employees.

WELCOME BACK: NOW WHAT?

Reality Check

Internal consultants can help foster the transfer of learning by clearly communicating to participants that new skills and knowledge are much easier to understand and apply in a training environment than when they are on the job. This important technique is referred to as *reality check.*

Managers and supervisors expect new skills and knowledge to be applied immediately; however, the reality is that such behavior cannot and will not occur easily. It takes a great deal of practice for new skills to be developed and a great deal of discipline to integrate new knowledge. Therefore, employees must be prepared for a period when it appeared that training was a waste of time. Internal consultants can be a great help by reminding employees of how difficult it is to transfer new skills and knowledge on the job.

Refresher Courses

Another effective activity internal consultants can provide after training is a short refresher course for participants. During refresher courses, participants could: (1) talk about the difficulties they are having with the integration of new skills and knowledge in the workplace, (2) identify barriers that prevent learning transfer, (3) share how they have incorporated new skills and knowledge in their particular situation, and (4) get reinforcement of the major learning points of the training program and intervention.

This type of dialogue greatly enhances transfer because it allows participants to find strategies that are successful as well as talk about things that prevent the transfer of learning. It also gives you the opportunity to reemphasize the key points of the training program or intervention by reminding employees of their importance and application. These sessions should be fairly short, perhaps two to three hours, but not more than a half day.

Performance Job Aids

Next, internal consultants should provide performance or job aids that allow for new skills and knowledge to be applied more easily. Such aids should be designed in a user-friendly and practical manner. It helps participants the most if you talk about training and performance aids at the end of a training program or intervention. This discussion points out that such aids exist. Refresher courses are also an excellent time to remind participants about job and performance aids.

Follow-Up Activities

Internal consultants can also aid in the transfer of learning by giving proper and prompt follow-up activities such as one-on-one interviews, which identify the successes and difficulties participants are having. While it is impossible to follow up with all participants, it is important to choose a sample of individuals and conduct these types of follow-up sessions. Individual and group follow-up sessions can also help you redesign training programs and interventions because they give you critical information about the success or failure of learning activities and the application of the course content.

Evaluation Strategies

Internal consultants should also conduct a proper evaluation after a training program or intervention. The most common form of evaluation, of course, is the reaction evaluation, often referred to as the *smile sheet*. This evaluation is usually conducted immediately following the training activity. This evaluation provides immediate feedback about what participants enjoyed the most or the least about the training program, but it does not give any information about the success or failure of learning transfer.

Therefore, internal consultants should also conduct behavioral evaluations that are designed to measure whether or not the proper behaviors occurred some time after the training program or intervention. Of course, depending on the type of training program or intervention, it may be equally important to conduct "impact evaluations." These measure the cost/benefit relationship of a training program or intervention. If such evaluations are required, they should be planned well in advance of the training program or intervention.

Regardless of which type of evaluation you use, you need to communicate to upper management about the success or failure of a training program or intervention. The more critical the skill or knowledge, the more important it is to identify a proper evaluation strategy and communicate the results.

Positive Reinforcement

Internal consultants must help managers and supervisors give the type of positive reinforcement that encourages participation in training programs and interventions. When managers and supervisors provide such supports for learning, employees are more willing to transfer new skills and knowledge to the workplace. Encourage managers and supervisors to allow their employees to practice new skills or integrate new knowledge on the job. This encouragement should also be a part of every follow-up and support activity that managers and supervisors give to their employees.

Failure Is a Learning Activity

Internal consultants have a difficult task of convincing managers and supervisors that new skills and knowledge may interfere with present skills or knowledge. This interference often confuses the learner, and productivity may slip for a short time. Managers and supervisors can get very nervous about this loss and be reluctant to continue supporting the acquisition of new skills and knowledge.

Thus, it is your responsibility to convince managers and supervisors that failure is a part of the learning process.

Participants who are allowed to fail in comfortable and supportive settings will learn a great deal about their current skill set and what will or will not work on the job. Learning failure often allows for a quicker, more accurate application of new skills and knowledge. Short-term gains are substituted for long-term successes. The natural results are skill application and knowledge integration. These helps employees increase their productivity and improve their job performance.

Role Models

Managers and supervisors must also understand that they are role models that employees look up to. It is an internal consultant's responsibility to convince management that being a role model is critical to transferring new skills and knowledge. By identifying individuals who demonstrate "best practices," internal consultants have, in essence, created a live performance/job aid that can be used by participants as a constant reminder of how new skills and knowledge can help them.

Performance Review and Appraisals

Internal consultants also have the responsibility of conveying to managers and supervisors the importance of integrating new skills and knowledge into performance reviews and appraisals. If management doesn't integrate them, employees will think the new skills and knowledge are not important and will not develop them to their fullest potential. A way of convincing managers and supervisors to do this activity is to tell them that a "behavior change will most likely occur around the things you inspect, rather than the things you expect." Therefore, if new skills and knowledge are worth obtaining, they are worth measuring.

Public Recognition

To greatly enhance the acquisition of new skills and knowledge, managers and supervisors should publicly recognize individuals who have reached a certain level of mastery. This activity, again, can be linked to performance standards identified before training. Recognition can also be used as a way to encourage self-development. This type of activity not only provides a positive environment for learning transfer, but it also improves the self-esteem of individuals who have taken the risk of acquiring new skills and knowledge. For this reason, participants should be encouraged to continue self-development activities.

Mentoring

A natural extension of role models is the development of mentoring relationships between managers and supervisors and their employees. In many organizations, this is referred to as the buddy system. In such a relationship, managers and supervisors are paired with employees immediately after training. Management's primary responsibility is to make certain that the new skills and knowledge are applied on the job. This relationship also gives an opportunity for managers and supervisors to develop better communication with employees.

Mentoring is a time-consuming process and requires a commitment by managers and supervisors who serve as mentors. Therefore, mentoring should not be taken lightly, because once begun, it must continue, to avoid negative consequences.

Daily Logs

Internal consultants can help employees develop daily logs designed to capture employees' progress in the development of new skills and knowledge. Such logs allow employees to document the circumstances and events surrounding the application of a specific skill or integration of knowledge. Employees should describe the circumstances and events in as much detail as possible. They should also describe the outcomes of the application or integration. Over time, daily logs will show the circumstances and events that enhance learning transfer, and those that do not.

Daily logs are also a form of "personal contracting," which encourages participants to record their daily progress. Internal consultants can use these logs to identify the barriers that may exist

Improving the Transfer of Learning

Barriers	Preparing for → Change	Training: Opportunities for → Improvement	Application and → Follow-Up
Type of:	Actions:	Actions:	Actions:
• Lack of reinforcement • Interference of tasks • Nonsupport environment • Pressure from peers • Negative perception of training by management and employees • Discomfort with change	• Solicit manager's, supervisor's and employees input • Orient managers and supervisors • Identify performance standards • Communicate management's support for training • Communicate importance of training • Identify rewards • Develop coaching skills	• Provide positive learning environment • Encourage participation • Provide practical learning experience • Develop learner's readiness to learn • Provide feedback • Provide job aids • Provide rewards and recognition • Create support groups on the job • Develop personal performance contracts	• Develop refresher courses • Provide job aids • Provide follow-up activities • Provide positive reinforcement • Understand failure is a learning activity • Develop role models • Conduct performance reviews • Provide public recognition • Develop mentoring activities • Use daily logs

within the organization which prevent learning transfer. In addition, daily logs serve as a constant reminder of the importance of the new skills and knowledge acquired and their application to the workplace.

Participant Responsibilities

Finally, you have the responsibility to communicate to participants that *they* are ultimately responsible for the transfer of learning. They must have the desire to manage themselves and the work environment to allow learning transfer. This level of self-discipline and management is not present in all participants, which is the reason transfer of learning does not occur for everyone. In fact, creating self-management and job management skills for employees is a full-time job for internal consultants. That's how important this activity is to successful learning transfer. We have illustrated the learning transfer concept at the end of this chapter.

Chapter Six

Using Strategic Planning to Improve Internal Consulting

You may wonder why it is important to create and implement a strategic plan for your HRD department. Perhaps the best example of the importance of planning was laid out in the book *Alice in Wonderland*. The following passage is taken from that book, and is an excellent example of the value of the planning process:

> *"Cheshire Puss," she began, rather timidly, and she did not at all know whether it would like the name: however, it only grinned a little wider. Come, it's pleased so far, thought Alice, and she went on. "Would you please tell me, please, which way I ought to go from here?"*
>
> *"That depends a good deal on where you want to get to," said the cat.*
>
> *"I don't much care where," said Alice.*
>
> *"Then it doesn't matter which way you go," said the cat.*
>
> *"So long as I get somewhere," Alice added as an explanation.*
>
> *"Oh, you're sure to do that," said the cat "if you only walk long enough."*
>
> (Lewis Carroll, Alice in Wonderland)

This passage illustrates the importance of planning. Without planning, you surely will end up somewhere, but it may not be where you want to go. And you may accomplish an outcome you don't desire.

The planning process is simply a systematic way of organizing the future. It helps you name the direction you want, define the outcomes you want, and find out how to get there.

WHY IS STRATEGIC PLANNING CRITICAL FOR INTERNAL CONSULTANTS?

Strategic planning is as much a philosophy as it is a plan. You should use strategic planning as a minute-by-minute, day-by-day process of planning and managing. Strategic planning should not merely be an exercise conducted once a year and then forgotten during the heat of battle. Strategic planning should be used as a tool to help you do more of the important things that are critical to your HRD program. Also, strategic planning should help you integrate the HRD program into the organization, to improve the organization's efficiency.

Many internal consultants use strategic planning to *develop a common purpose or focus among HRD professionals.*

Strategic planning also helps internal HRD consultants *improve their credibility within the organization.* This happens when you analyze client needs and gather information about their perceptions of the organization and its operations. When you conduct this analysis, you show your willingness to listen to your clients and demonstrate your problem-solving focus. These qualities enhance your credibility with your clients and improve relationships and communication.

Strategic planning also helps provide internal consultants with *an analysis of the organizational culture and the strengths and weaknesses of the HRD programs.* It gives a snapshot of the current opportunities available for HRD and the barriers to improvement. This information helps you decide which HRD programs to offer.

Another advantage of strategic planning is that it allows you to *develop a common set of goals and objectives* by which to carry out your operational missions. These goals and objectives should guide the steps to carry out the strategic plan. In other words, strategic plans provide internal consultants with a game plan for improving employee performance and organizational effectiveness.

Finally, strategic planning is *a long-term, decision-making activity designed to foster change within the organization.* It requires the committed effort of all HRD professionals and internal HRD consultants. In many ways, strategic planning is a team-building strategy because it forces the HRD staff to collectively analyze the organization's culture, identify the program's missions, develop program goals and objectives, and select plans for change.

Perhaps the best definition, then, of the strategic planning process is it helps you identify and keep a *focus* for the HRD program, using past experience as a filter for future decisions.[1] Strategic planning helps you focus your attention on the outcomes you desire: improving the organization.

SEVEN STEPS TO STRATEGIC PLANNING

Strategic planning consists of seven separate, but interrelated, steps. They include:

1. Identify organizational values.
2. Create an operational mission statement.
3. Conduct environmental analysis (internal and external).
4. Identify goals and objectives.
5. Identify action steps to carry out the plan.
6. Conduct reality testing of the plan.
7. Obtain feedback (see Figure 6–1).

1. Identifying Organizational Values

Strategic planning begins with identifying the values that are critical to the organization, because those values directly influence how people behave. During this phase of the strategic planning process, you should identify the feelings, beliefs, and attitudes of employees and organization decision-makers. The composite of these values makes up the "organizational culture." According to Ron Galbraith, president of Management 21, "the organizational culture is perhaps the most powerful internal force affecting any organization."

Organizational culture defines expectations about behavior,

FIGURE 6–1
Strategic Planning Process

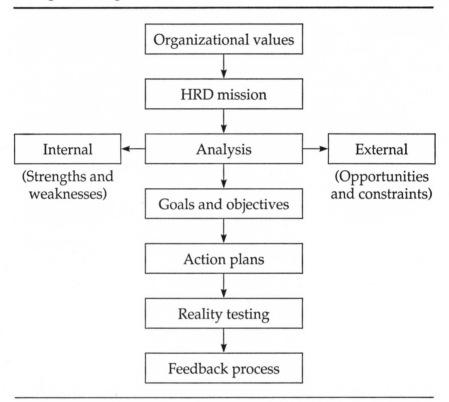

how work is done, how decisions are made, how social interactions are structured, and how people communicate.[2] Therefore, strategic planning in HRD must consider each of these parts of the organizational culture. These organizational values will serve as a guide in your decision-making.

Another important part of identifying organizational values is to name the roles that leaders play in developing and keeping the organizational culture. You can do this by interviewing a number of organizational leaders to hear their insights about how the organizational culture evolved and continues today. It is important to show the leaders' roles in this process, as well as to identify other outside influences on organizational values.

You may want to begin the interviews with a list of questions you will ask each leader. It is just as important to give these individuals an opportunity to expand their ideas as it is to let them share information they believe is critical to developing an organizational culture. This two-phased approach to interviewing will enable you to gather consistent information from person to person, while allowing for individual perceptions and beliefs about the organization and its culture.

Interview questions may include the following:

1. What are your expectations about behavior of employees?
2. What are your performance expectations of those employees?
3. How are decisions made within the organization?
4. How should people communicate within the organization?
5. How should work be accomplished within the organization?
6. What is quality?
7. How can the organization improve its performance and efficiency?
8. What type of social interaction should be allowed within the organization?

Each of these questions helps you identify the organizational leaders' perceptions of the work process, performance improvement criteria, quality issues, and interpersonal interaction—the organization's "values."

2. Identifying the HRD Mission

The next step in the strategic planning process is to identify a mission, which gives you a sense of purpose and direction. The HRD mission should be compared to the organization's mission statement to make sure the HRD mission reflects the organization's direction.

Robert Dean, director of HRD at the Humana Corporation, believes an HRD mission statement can:

• Help organize other HRD professionals within the organization around a common outcome.

- Serve as a guide to help internal consultants in decision-making.
- Focus the role of the HRD program within the organization.
- Communicate the type of HRD interventions and strategies necessary to improve the effectiveness, profitability, and competitiveness of the organization.
- Serve as a guide to developing goals and objectives for the HRD program.

When creating a mission statement, you must include five things:

1. The name of your group.
2. The role that HRD practitioners will serve in the organization (internal consultant, trainer, instructional designer, etc.).
3. The type of population served.
4. The type of interventions to be used by HRD programs.
5. The type of outcomes desired because of the intervention.

In 1990, the American Society for Training and Development (ASTD) developed a book series called *Trainer's Tool Kit*. One of the first books to be published in this series was titled *Mission Statements for HRD Programs*. This book included sample mission statements from a number of different organizations.[3] Let's look at one of the mission statements and see if it consists of the five important components previously identified.

"William M. Mercer, Incorporated: The Corporate Professional Development group provides internal consulting services to enhance performance for individuals and groups. We do this through the application of performance interventions which enhance employee satisfaction and growth, and improve efficiency, competitiveness and profitability (page 143)."

Let's analyze this mission statement to decide if each of the five components exists. The name of the group in this example was a "professional development group." They perceived their role within the organization as "internal consultants." They broadly identified their population as "individuals and groups within the organization." They identified "performance interventions" as

Example

Many HRD departments have a difficult time resisting the requests made by organizational members because HRD professionals understand that their worth and credibility are directly linked to the perceptions of executives, managers, and supervisors. Therefore, we are always saying yes even when it confuses the image of HRD within the organization.

Recently, an HRD professional of a large management consulting firm was facing this dilemma. The department was small in comparison to the organization. It consisted of three senior-level internal consultants reporting to the executive vice president of professional development, three instructional designers, two material developers, one conference design manager, and five conference planners and meeting coordinators. The senior-level internal consultants were the only staff members delivering training programs. All three had Ph.Ds in HRD or adult education.

The organization consisted of 3,500 employees with 2,000 middle- and senior-level consultants. The remaining 1,500 employees were researchers, analysts, technical professionals, and support staff. This audience also received training from the senior-level internal consultants.

As you can see, the HRD staff was very lean, with little time for activities other than those that were HRD-related. It was discovered, however, that one of the senior internal consultants was accepting external consulting assignments with clients. While this provided revenue for the organization, it was creating an image problem for the HRD program within the organization. It also caused serious workload inequities among the senior-level internal consultants.

This situation was discussed during a quarterly staff meeting of the senior staff and its boss (executive vice president). It was finally decided that the HRD program was funded and supported to address the professional and organizational needs of the company. Therefore, the internal consultants would no longer accept external assignments, even though they produced needed revenue.

The internal consultants created a mission statement that allowed them to examine similar requests. This decision helped them keep the correct focus. It also gave the internal consultant who was accepting external assignments an "excuse" to refuse future requests without offending senior management.

A mission statement allows internal consultants and HRD professionals to agree on a common approach. It also helps resolve conflicts and provides direction for less senior staff members. Finally, a mission statement organizes the activities of internal consultants and HRD professionals.

their primary approach to be used within the organization. This approach could include training, organizational development activities, change interventions, and a variety of other approaches. They identified their outcomes as "employee satisfaction and growth, and improved efficiency, competitiveness and profitability."

In this example, all five components are included in this mission statement. You can see how these five criteria help in writing a clear and concise mission statement. It is clear who is represented, their role, the population served, the interventions used, and the desired outcomes.

Developing a mission statement is a soul-searching and time-consuming process. Each member of the HRD program will have a different view of what the program is about and what it should be about. However, it is essential that all HRD members ultimately agree with the mission of the program and support it. A well-defined mission statement gives everyone a sense of purpose, direction, significance, and achievement. A mission statement acts as an invisible hand that guides widely scattered practitioners to work independently and yet collectively toward the HRD programs' goals.[4]

3. Internal and External Environmental Analysis

The third step in setting up a strategic plan for HRD programs is conducting an internal and external environmental analysis. This step will help you find your strengths and weaknesses (internal) and opportunities and constraints (external). Another purpose of this analysis is to determine which contingencies will help or prevent you from carrying out the programs' mission. From this analysis, you can make adjustments to compensate for constraints and weaknesses.

Internal environmental analysis considers the organization's financial condition, managerial abilities and attitudes, facilities, staff size and quality, competitive position, image, and structure. External environmental analysis considers the economic condition of the organization, legal and political realities, social and cultural values, the state of technology, availability of resources, and the competitive structure of the organization.

FIGURE 6–2
Suggested Variables for Analyzing the Internal Environment

Internal Environmental Analysis

Strengths/Weakenesses

1. Financial condition of organization:

2. Managerial attitudes and abilities:

3. Present facilities:

4. Personnel quality and quantity:

5. HRD's competitive positions:

6. HRD's organizational image:

7. Centralized versus decentralized structure:

Internal environmental analysis. Examining your internal environment will help you find your strengths and weaknesses, which can affect how well you carry out your mission. Based on this analysis, you should adjust your efforts to recognize and eliminate weaknesses in the HRD program and take advantage of the strengths that exist within the program.

The internal environment of an organization may consist of as many as four groups of people: the organization's board of directors, management, staff or employees, and any volunteers and consultants with close associations to the organization.

Figure 6–2 names the seven parts of an internal environmental analysis:

1. Financial condition of organization.
2. Managerial attitudes and abilities.
3. Present facilities.
4. Personnel quality and quantity.
5. HRD's competitive positions.
6. HRD's organizational image.
7. Centralized versus decentralized structure.

These items can be used to identify the strengths and weaknesses of the HRD program and the organization as it relates to each of these topics. You can use this form to construct an interview, develop a questionnaire, or conduct observations of the HRD program to show the strengths and weaknesses of the practitioners, the program, and the organization. Steve Merman, vice president of King, Chapman, Borussard, and Gallagher, believes the information gathered should be used to allocate human and financial resources for the HRD program and to further develop a strategic approach for the program.

External environmental analysis.   You conduct an external environmental analysis to determine the opportunities facing an organization and the constraints placed on it. An external environmental analysis can provide a long-term report of the condition of the organization about:

1. Economic conditions.
2. Legal-political environment.
3. Sociocultural values.
4. Technological state.
5. Resource availability.
6. Competitive structures (see Figure 6–3).

This information is important because it reveals the economic health of the organization, its values, political climate, and uses of technology and resources. Each of these provides internal consultants with a wealth of information that can be used to make decisions and allocate resources. Once you identify the opportunities and/or constraints facing an organization in each of these six areas, you have information that is critical to the long-term health of the organization. The external analysis also supplies necessary infor-

FIGURE 6–3
Suggested Variables for Analyzing the External Environment

External Environmental Analysis

Opportunities/Constraints

1. Economic conditions:

2. Legal-political environment:

3. Sociocultural values:

4. Technological state:

5. Resource availability:

6. Competitive structures:

---

mation about the critical financial and human resources available for the expansion and growth of an HRD program.

Another important part of an external environmental analysis is identifying the current technological state of the organization and its plans for research and development. The type of technology available can have a major impact on the change interventions used in your HRD program. If the organization is behind in technology, this fact may limit your attempts to improve the organization's effectiveness and profitability. This, in turn, could be very critical to the long-term success of HRD.

4. Goals and Objectives

Once you have identified the values for an organization, developed the mission statement, and conducted the internal and external environmental analyses, it is time to begin developing strategic goals and objectives. The HRD mission statements suggest where the program is coming from, while the goals and objectives indicate where it is going.[5]

The goals and objectives of HRD programs can vary from year to year, depending on the problems and issues facing the organization. The purpose of each goal and objective, however, is to carry out the broader mission of the HRD program. Colvin Henderson, manager of human resources for William M. Mercer, Incorporated's Office of Information and Technology, believes that internal consultants who don't filter their goals and objectives through the HRD mission will find themselves off course and will realize that they are engaged in activities they were not intended or qualified to do.

Goals. Many internal consultants think it is easy to set goals; you just state them. But it is not easy. It is hard work. It is also one of the most important actions you can take to improve the strategic focus of an HRD program.

What does it take to set a good strategic goal? In setting a strategic goal, you are trying to do two things:

1. Focusing yourself, your clients, and your team on the target.
2. Creating commitment and agreement about the HRD program's strategic goals.

An effectively written strategic goal should have five characteristics: specific, measurable, agreed upon, realistic, and written.

1. **Specific:** Your strategic goal statement should be so specific, well-defined, and clear that anyone with some basic knowledge of an HRD program can read it, understand it, and know what you are trying to do.
2. **Measurable:** To manage an HRD program successfully, you must be able to measure how well the program meets the goal. Every strategic goal can be measured; it is just that some goals can be measured more easily than others. In fact, you'll spend the most time developing clear, measurable standards for the more ambiguous and fuzzy types of goals. Without measurable goals, members of

your HRD team cannot get any sense of accomplishment.

Some recommended standards that can be used in measuring any goal are quantity, quality, time, and cost. Each of these variables can be used to help you write strategic goals that are measurable.

For example, you could write a goal that incorporates two or more of these variables. Let us illustrate: "During the next fiscal year (time), our Supervisory Management Program will be delivered to 20 percent (quantity) of sales division's supervisors. The month after training (time), supervisors will participate in simulation designed to determine their level of mastery of supervisory skills (quality)."

In this example, we used three of the four variables: time, quantity, and quality. When you're deciding whether or not you've reached your goal, these variables will help provide solid evidence of your success.

3. **Agreed Upon:** You and other members of the HRD team must agree on the strategic goals of the HRD program. The team must agree that the result should solve the problem or respond to the need that led to the intervention in the first place. The more the team agrees and clarifies the goal up front, the easier it will be to develop a plan of action for the HRD program. This agreement will also make it easier to respond to changes that may require changing the goal as the program unfolds. Agreement is based on shared information, and it builds commitment to the HRD program.

4. **Realistic:** Strategic goals must be realistic. All too often internal consultants set goals that are impossible to achieve given the resources and time available. Unrealistic goals only set you and your programs up for frustration and failure. Making the goal realistic may mean adjusting the goal, deadline, or resources.

In the previous example, we identified a 20 percent saturation level during a one-year period. This figure appears to be a realistic level of participation. If we had identified a saturation level of 85 percent, it may not be as realistic, given your resources and capacity to deliver the program. On the other hand, an 85 percent level could be realistic if you have the resources to reach the goal. That's why it's important to develop goals based on the size, availability, and skills of your HRD practitioners.

5. **Written:** All strategic goals should be written. This will help you better articulate the desired outcomes for your HRD program and remain focused during difficult economic and stressful periods within the organization. Written strategic goals also improve commitment from you and your clients.

Objectives. Strategic goals help you decide where the program is headed. Objectives, on the other hand, help you identify *how* a strategic goal is to be implemented.

Objectives are similar to goals, but they are focused on the subparts of the HRD program. Objectives break down the strategic goals into a set of specific tasks. They tell each group what to do, when to do it, and how to measure progress. Accomplishing all of the objectives leads to the overall strategic goal.

Objectives focus on the details and tell you more about what specific people need to do. They set a target for each of the various people or groups involved in an HRD program.

Just as with goals, objectives must be specific, measurable, agreed upon, realistic, and written; otherwise, strategic objectives cannot effectively guide your behavior.

Once you have a clear statement of the strategic objectives, you need to name the key participants and resources necessary to carry out the overall strategic goal. Continuing with our previous example, we can identify the human and financial resources needed to carry out each objective. We can also identify the participants for the training program.

You will establish "ownership" in the objectives by naming and discussing each objective with a specific group (or a specific individual). Ownership leads people to take responsibility and feel committed to carrying out the objective.

Having clear strategic goals and objectives is essential to effective HRD programs and effective performance of HRD practitioners. According to Gloria Regalbuto, president of Seacorp University, division of Seacorp Bank in Seattle, research on peak performers suggests that these people are always clear about their goals and objectives. They know where they are headed. It is this sense of direction that substantially increases their chances of getting there.

5. Action Plans

An integral part of strategic planning is to develop an action plan for implementing all goals and objectives. This action plan should address two basic issues:

1. What are the possible problem areas in implementing the strategic plan?
2. How will new strategies be developed if the main plan begins to go astray?

The purpose of this step is to ensure that the strategic plan actually gets implemented. You must consider several important issues when you are developing this phase of a strategic plan:

1. How will the comprehensive strategic plan be implemented?
2. Who will be in charge of implementing it?
3. What is the basic timetable for implementation?
4. How will the success of achieving a plan be measured?[6]

An action plan is critical to the success of the strategic planning process because it is what "drives" the process. And the actual steps involved in creating an action plan are driven by the strategic goals and objectives.

6. Reality Testing

While you're creating your strategic plan, you may become so future-oriented and visionary that you lose touch with day-to-day reality. To prevent the strategic planning process from becoming unrealistic, it is important to answer the following question, "Are our strategic goals and objectives realistic and attainable, given the real constraints of our situation?"

During the reality-testing phase, keep in mind the following:

1. What resources do we need to accomplish our goals and objectives and fulfill our mission?

2. If the needed resources do not exist, can they be acquired or created?
3. Who can help us get these resources?
4. What are the important constraints that might keep us from carrying out our goals and objectives?
5. Is it possible to decrease these constraints? How?[7]

Wendy Lawson, director of executive development at Marietta Corporation, believes that, "the reality testing phase is the last opportunity for internal consultants to modify their mission, goals, and objectives before implementing the strategic plan."

Therefore, it is absolutely critical that you conduct a reality test on the strategic plan before implementing it. This test will help ensure the success of the strategic plan.

7. Feedback System

The last part of the strategic planning process is creating a feedback system that provides you with results of your strategic plan. The feedback system gives information about the success or failure of the strategic plan, to help in designing future strategic plans that are better targeted to carrying out a desired result.

One way to develop a feedback system is to find the answers to the following important questions:

1. How will you know when the strategic goals and objectives have been accomplished?
2. What type of early warning system can be created to tell you of impending problems?
3. What alternative plans can be created if the first plan fails?
4. How can you avoid punishing people if the plan does not accomplish its outcome?
5. How will people be rewarded if you successfully achieve your goals and objectives?
6. How will you check the progress of your strategic plan?
7. Who will be in charge of periodically checking on the implementation of the strategic plan?

FIGURE 6–4
Strategic Planning Process

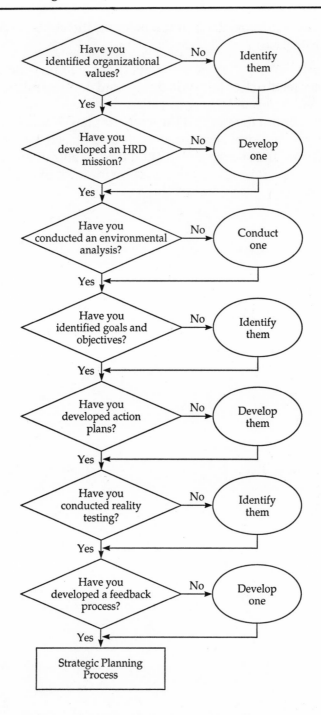

8. How will progress in implementing the strategic plan be
   measured?

The answers to each of these questions will provide you with
necessary feedback to help you design and develop future strategic
plans (see Figure 6–4).

It is important to note that the strategic plan should be designed
to help you accomplish desired goals and objectives for a *specific
period*. Then, the strategic plan should be analyzed and changed,
as necessary. Strategic planning is ongoing; it should not be a
one-time effort.

Chapter Seven

Applying the Marketing Process to Enhance Credibility

Marketing your HRD program is an important activity. It is a tool that can be used to improve the image, credibility, and acceptance of HRD. The ultimate goal of marketing is to integrate HRD into the fabric of the organization. If this is accomplished, HRD will become an equal partner with other essential parts of the organization such as finance, accounting, and operations.[1]

To develop a marketing approach, you must begin to think strategically by systematically organizing the future using past experiences as a filter for future decisions. Strategic thinking can be used to identify the actions required to change the image of HRD and the opportunities available for HRD within an organization.

Strategic thinking requires internal consultants to become proactive rather than reactive. You must become an active member of the management team and position yourself properly within the organization. If you want to have credibility, you must convince management that it can improve the competitiveness and effectiveness of the organization.

A strategic marketing plan for HRD within the organization will give you the tool to enhance your credibility. Creating the plan will require you to identify your priorities and improve your planning. Strategic marketing planning can help you conduct a better internal analysis that will identify the strengths and weaknesses of your program. This process will ultimately produce a series of marketing strategies that can be integrated and implemented within the organization.

THE STRATEGIC MARKETING PLANNING PROCESS

Strategic marketing planning consists of several integrated steps that lead to an action plan you can use. Each of these steps has as their foundation the critical laws of marketing: (1) the marketing concept, (2) the exchange process, and (3) the adoption process. Internal consultants must understand and apply each of these foundational laws before they begin strategic marketing planning.

The Marketing Concept

Internal consultants who adopt a service-oriented attitude, one that places client's needs and wants above their own, have begun to lay the proper foundation for strategic marketing planning. This attitude means you listen to your clients and work with them to identify organizational, professional, and personal needs.

A service-oriented attitude is not used to manipulate clients, but it is focused on discussing the performance problems and developmental concerns of the client and the organization. As a result, you can design training programs and other interventions to meet your clients' expressed interests and needs. One way to create a service-oriented attitude is to conduct an "internal audit" of yourself using "reflective activities."[2] You can begin by writing down *why* you are currently involved in the HRD field. Once you have completed a comprehensive list, try to isolate the essential theme. This written statement will give you a good understanding of your primary motive for being identified in HRD within your organization. In other words, it will help you figure out your marketing attitude.

Another way to figure out your marketing attitude is to conduct an informal group discussion with key members of the organization. This discussion should be designed to provide a free exchange of opinions, ideas, and beliefs about your role in the organization. This free exchange allows essential organizational members to communicate directly with you about their perception of your HRD efforts.

A more formal approach would be to conduct a focus group (described in Chapter 3), to identify essential themes, attitudes, and expectations. This process can produce critical information about the participant's feelings and attitudes toward HRD and internal consultants.

You can also conduct personal interviews to figure out your marketing attitude. This information will allow you to identify performance problems and developmental needs of your clients, and it can be used when you are developing future training programs and interventions designed to improve organizational effectiveness.

In addition, personal interviews allow a free exchange of opinions, ideas, and beliefs about the purpose and mission of the HRD program. The exchange also gives you the opportunity to further develop personal relationships with critical organizational leaders. These relationships can be extremely helpful in promoting HRD within the organization. Organizational leaders can become essential internal advocates for the HRD program.

The marketing concept should not be adopted in an attempt to manipulate or coerce organizational leaders. It should be adopted because it makes sense. It makes sense to place the needs and wants of your clients above your own needs and wants. It makes sense to communicate that the HRD program is designed and developed to improve performance and organizational effectiveness. It makes sense to focus your attention on organizational objectives and outcomes rather than on the objectives and outcomes of a given training program.

The marketing concept also makes sense because people support the activities and programs they are allowed to influence and impact. It is very important that you strongly consider the thoughts and feelings of organizational members before you develop any training program or other intervention.

The Exchange Process

The exchange process is defined as "offering value to another in return for equal or greater value." Training programs and interventions developed by HRD professionals must be viewed by the client as at least equal in value to the time, energy, and personal commitment exchanged for them.[3]

If the benefits to be received from the HRD program are viewed as greater than or equal to the time, energy, or personal commitment required from a client, an exchange will take place. If, however, the benefits received from HRD are not viewed in this way, an exchange will not take place.

While this is a reasonably simple concept, it is often overlooked by internal consultants when they try to communicate the values and benefits of their training programs and interventions. It is also one of the primary reasons why HRD programs are not perceived as critical components in the organization.

If internal consultants focus their attention on communicating the values and benefits of their training programs and interventions to their clients, the communication will create more exchange opportunities. As the number of exchanges increases, the opportunity to positively impact the organization increases accordingly. The more positive exchanges that occur, the more favorably HRD is viewed.

For example, suppose an internal consultant offers a time management training program to a critical client group. Figure 7–1 illustrates how the exchange process could work. The process begins with offering a training program (time management) that will provide improved time management techniques and personal productivity. The client group receives information about the time management program and the values they will receive.

A negotiation then occurs between the internal consultant and the client group. This negotiation focuses on the values received (time management techniques and improved personal productivity) in exchange for the client's time, effort, and personal commitment. If the client group perceives that the values offered are of greater benefit than what they are exchanging, they will agree to take part in the time management program. If the time management program provides the benefits desired, the exchange would be positive.

As a result of this positive exchange, the HRD program and the internal consultant will receive enhanced credibility in the eyes of the client group. This, in turn, will enhance the image of HRD.

The type of value being exchanged here must be carefully considered. Internal consultants must examine the outcomes of their interventions to decide if the results claimed can be accomplished. Once you determine the value to be exchanged, it must be communicated to the identified audience. The audience will look at the

FIGURE 7–1
Exchange Process: Time Management Training Program

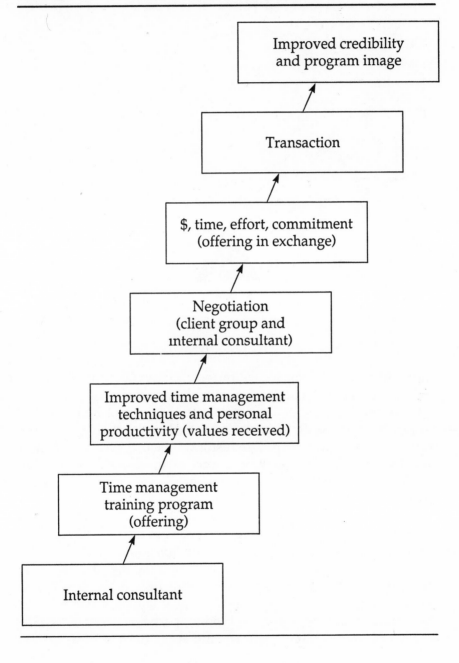

FIGURE 7–2
Value Equation

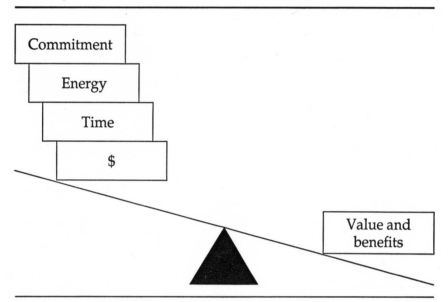

Source: Gilley, Jerry W. and Eggland, Steven A. *Marketing HRD Within Organizations: Enhancing the Visibility, Effectiveness, and Credibility of Programs*, Figure 2.2, p.32. © 1992 by Jossey-Bass Publishers.

offer and decide if they are willing to exchange their time, effort, and commitment to change for the value received.

If internal consultants communicate values and benefits that cannot be realized as a result of an exchange, clients will take part under false pretenses. The result will be disenchantment and dissatisfaction with the exchange, and it will adversely impact the image of HRD within the organization as well as cast negative dispersions on internal consultants.

As negotiations continue, clients will be weighing the cost of participating (time, effort, or commitment to change) against the value received (time management principles and increased personal productivity). This process is known as the *value equation* (see Figure 7–2). An exchange will occur only if the benefits of participating outweigh the cost. The value equation depends on the clients' willingness to attend (time), participate and engage in activities and role-playing (effort), and apply the concepts learned (commitment). For clients, the decision to take part is based on the perceived value of this type of exchange.

As you can see, communication is an important tool in the exchange process. Internal consultants must communicate the purpose, value, and impact of training programs and interventions, as well as identify their long-range results. If internal consultants successfully represent and communicate the values of training programs and interventions, an exchange will take place that will enhance the credibility of the HRD program.

The Adoption Process

The adoption process consists of five stages: (1) becoming aware of performance problems and developmental needs, (2) developing interest in solutions, (3) evaluating alternatives, (4) selecting an alternative, and (5) adopting an alternative and evaluating the choice.[4] Each time clients choose to take part in a training program or intervention, they engage in this decision-making process. Sometimes their decisions are simple and routine and require little effort; at other times they are difficult and complex and require a great deal of time and effort.

Step 1: Becoming aware of needs. People choose to take part in training programs and interventions for a variety of reasons. Usually, they have a knowledge or skill deficiency that affects their performance. This deficiency can greatly impede the career progress of the person and create considerable work frustration.

It is important to remember that performance problems differ in their degree of severity and urgency. Some need immediate attention, while others need little more than identification. Because of limited resources, internal consultants can only react to a selected number of client requests. Therefore, you must rank them.

One way is to consider the importance of each request in relationship to its urgency. Figure 7–3 illustrates how this can be done. First, the importance of each request must be evaluated. You must then decide if the request should be addressed immediately or if it can be delayed. Client requests that are both highly important and urgent are considered priorities. They must be addressed immediately, and large amounts of time should be spent completing them.

FIGURE 7–3
Determining Priorities

	Yes	Importance	No
Yes	Priority		Routine
Urgency			
No	Futuristic		Time waster

Requests that are less important but still urgent are considered routine. These requests must be a part of your daily routine. However, you need to limit routine activities because of the limited amount of time you have available. Requests that are highly important but not urgent are often referred to as futuristic. These requests have future implications on productivity as well as performance. Therefore, these requests should be a part of your long-term program offerings, but offer them at some point. If you do not, you can greatly damage the credibility and image of HRD.

Finally, requests that are low in importance and urgency are considered time wasters. Internal consultants should avoid spending valuable time on them.

Step 2: Developing interest. Once clients have identified their performance problems and developmental needs, they begin the "information gathering" phase of the adoption process. During this phase, clients begin to develop interest in the training programs and interventions designed to help them. Many clients are very active and involved in their search for information. They are referred to as "determined information seekers." These people will use any source of information to acquire additional knowledge about their problems and developmental interests.

There are also "passive" information seekers. They are more casual and informal in their quest for information. Many times, passive information seekers rely on the opinions of others about the effectiveness and value of training programs and interventions they are considering.

Regardless of the type of information seeker, the clients become much more focused as the complexity of a decision increases. As an internal consultant, your task is to help your clients better understand the values and benefits of each of the training programs and interventions you offer. Second, you must communicate your professional experience as well as show examples of your work for them to see. This activity will demonstrate your credibility. You are responsible for educating your client about the products and services you can provide and how you can best deliver them to the organization.

Step 3: Evaluating alternatives.   Once clients have gathered information about the training programs and interventions available to meet their needs, they must assess the programs and identify alternatives. We believe there are several steps needed to carry out this task (see Figure 7–4).

The process can best be illustrated by an example. At the beginning of each year, the professional development committee of William M. Mercer, Incorporated, introduces its HRD programs to its consultants. Consultants are required to choose two courses to take part in during the year.

First, each consultant receives an HRD catalog outlining all possible training programs offered. The catalog includes the name of each program, its outline, learning objectives, advantages and benefits, the training methods and activities involved, the time requirements, offering dates and locations. This listing of all possibilities is known as the *total set*; it includes 11 training programs.

The total set can be divided into two categories: the "awareness set," consisting of the programs with which the consultants are familiar; and the "unawareness set," consisting of those with which they are not familiar. The awareness set can be a very short list if the consultants are not familiar with the training programs offered through HRD.

At this point, all training programs are still being considered, but the consultants will only seriously consider a limited number. This group represents the "consideration set." The other training programs are relegated to an "infeasible set."

FIGURE 7–4
Evaluating Programs and Services: The Process of Evaluation

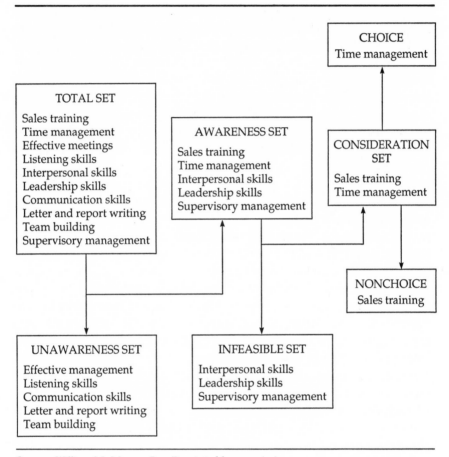

Source: William M. Mercer, Inc. Reprinted by permission.

While consultants have gathered additional information about the training programs in the consideration set, a few remain of greater interest. These form the "choice set"; the remainder are placed in the "nonchoice set." The last phase is a careful evaluation of the choice sets, followed by a final selection, referred to as a "decision."[5]

Step 4: Selecting an alternative. Selecting a training program or intervention is often as simple as evaluating alternatives.

Several factors, however, may influence the selection of an alternative. First, the attitudes of others may greatly impact the choice made by clients. For example, if a training program is not positively perceived by others within the organization, participation will be limited. The attitudes of others toward HRD in general can also impact participation in HRD offerings. Therefore, the reputation of HRD within the organization is extremely critical. It should be protected by internal consultants at all times.

Second, some training programs and interventions require clients to undertake greater amounts of psychological and physical risks. Under these circumstances, the values and benefits received must outweigh the risks to be taken. If they don't, an exchange most likely will not occur.

Third, the previous experiences clients have had with training programs and interventions will greatly impact their future participation. If the experiences have been positive, clients will more likely take part in future programs. However, if the experiences have been negative, clients may avoid taking part to prevent a reoccurrence of the negative experience.

Fourth, the attitudes clients have toward learning influences whether or not they will participate in training programs and interventions. Attitudes are very difficult to change. Many of the clients' attitudes are directly related to their experiences with HRD in general. But also, many clients have a predispensation to self-development. Those clients who are positively predisposed will most likely participate in greater numbers of training programs and interventions. Those who are negatively predisposed will most likely avoid taking part in training programs and interventions.

Regardless of the reasons that influence a client's selection, internal consultants must be proactive in communicating the values and benefits of the training programs and interventions. The previous experiences and attitudes of your clients toward training should be considered when you communicate the positive aspects of participating in HRD programs. Communication based on your clients background and interest will greatly improve their involvement in HRD programs.

Step 5: Evaluating the selection. Many clients have second thoughts after making a decision to take part in training programs or interventions. This condition is known as "postdecision dissonance." It is tension created by uncertainty about the decision's correctness.[6] The person wonders if another alternative would have been a better choice. This condition can often distort the satisfaction level clients experience related to their choice.

Postdecision dissonance often occurs when clients feel abandoned by trainers after the course ends. This condition can easily be overcome by providing appropriate follow-up activities that reinforce learning.

After a training program or intervention, most clients experience some level of satisfaction or dissatisfaction. This outcome is often referred to as "expectation-performance theory."[7] According to this theory, the client's level of satisfaction is directly related to their expectation of how the learning will be used. If their expectations are met, the clients are very satisfied. However, if their expectations are not met, they will be dissatisfied.

For example, a person may take part in a sales training course and learn the techniques of selling. However, if the participant tries to apply these techniques in real life and they don't work, dissatisfaction with the training course results.

Internal consultants can prevent postdecision dissonance and dissatisfaction by withholding claims about their training programs or interventions that cannot be realized. This type of careful communication can help prevent clients from setting up high expectations that cannot be met through the HRD program.

You can conduct focus groups and/or client interviews to decide if the training programs and interventions offered are meeting expectations. These discussions will help you decide whether or not the values and benefits received from training are equal to or greater than the time, effort, and personal commitment required, because you are focusing your attention on the exchange process.

If you have developed a proper attitude toward your clients, incorporated the exchange process into your daily interactions with clients, and used the five-step adoption process to help decision-making, you have started laying the proper foundation for strategic marketing planning. Each of these components can strengthen and improve strategic marketing planning. However, the absence of any of these three foundational components will severely weaken your ability to create a strategic marketing plan.

SIX STEPS TO STRATEGIC MARKETING PLANNING

The goal of strategic marketing planning is to help you maximize exchanges within the organization. More positive exchanges between your HRD programs and employees help improve client satisfaction and quality and will enable you and the HRD program to gain greater respect and an improved image.

The strategic marketing planning process consists of six steps:

1. Mission (why).
2. Operational analysis (barriers).
3. Goals (outcomes).
4. Target market (who).
5. Marketing mix (how).
6. Integration and implementation (action) (see Figure 7–5).

The strategic planning and strategic marketing planning process consist of the same first three steps. We briefly overview those before we describe the last three steps.

Mission

As we discussed in Chapter 6, creating a mission statement is a soul-searching and time-consuming process. Many internal consultants within HRD differ in their views of what HRD is about or what it should be about. It is important, however, that each internal consultant ultimately agree with the overall program's mission and support it accordingly.

One of the best ways for internal consultants to create a mission statement is to answer these questions: (1) What is your purpose? (2) Who are your customers? (3) What is the value to your customers? (4) What should your purpose be? (5) What will your purpose be in the future?

Refer to Chapter 6 for more information on mission statements.

Operational Analysis

The second step in setting up a strategic marketing plan is to conduct a working analysis. In strategic planning terms, this is often

FIGURE 7–5
Strategic Planning Process

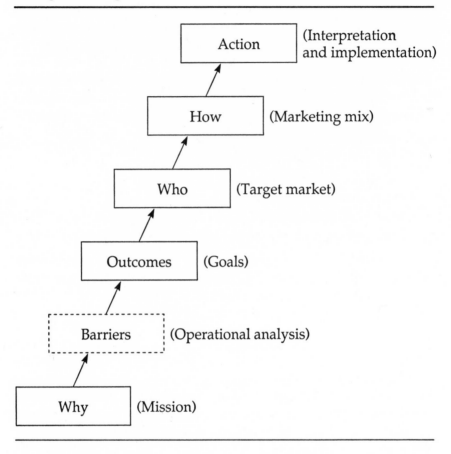

referred to as the internal and external environmental analysis. Refer to Chapter 6 for details on these analyses.

HRD Program Goals

Once you have developed the HRD mission and conducted a working analysis, it is time to develop HRD program goals. By identifying clear and concise goals, you will set the direction and focus of your HRD program. We believe that setting goals provides a superstructure for the rest of the strategic marketing planning process.

Remember that HRD program goals can vary from year to year, depending on the perception of critical problems facing internal consultants. The purpose of HRD program goals should be to accomplish the broader mission of the program. You must filter your goals through your mission or you may find yourself off course.

When creating goals for the HRD program, you should consider the following characteristics: goals should be specific, measurable, agreed upon, realistic, and written.

Refer to Chapter 6 for more information on setting goals.

Target Market

When constructing a strategic marketing plan, it is extremely important that you name the people who will have the greatest potential of being impacted and influenced. This group is referred to as the *target market*.

The first step in deciding the proper target market is to understand the term *market*. A market is a group of people who have an actual or potential interest in the products or services offered and have the ability to pay for those products and services. Although there are various "market segments," it is important to remember that the target market is the group of individuals who you have the greatest ability to impact or influence.

By identifying the target market, you can decide which training program or intervention can have the greatest impact on your clients. In this way, you can improve client satisfaction and enhance client relationships. Remember, you must make decisions about how to allocate and use limited resources. Therefore, it is extremely critical to focus your attention on the market segments that will produce the best results for the HRD program.

The Marketing Mix

Having named the most appropriate target market, your next task is to identify the marketing mix. A marketing mix consists of four kinds of strategies designed to help the HRD program carry out its objectives. They include: (1) program/service strategy, (2) cost/benefit strategy, (3) time/location strategy, and (4) promotional strategy.

Program/service strategy. A program/service strategy is designed to help internal consultants name the training programs and interventions that have the greatest potential for changing the organization and its clients. This strategy helps you identify the importance and application of each training program intervention offered. This information can then be used to help you allocate human and financial resources. It will also supply other information necessary for you to request additional support for ever-increasing training demands.

In this way, you are ranking your training programs and interventions to increase your efficiency. As a result, you can apply one of four strategic decisions to each training program or intervention: to build, to hold, to harvest, or to divest.

1. **To build**—This decision often means committing additional financial and human resources to develop or improve a training program or intervention. A build strategy should be reserved for only those programs or interventions that have the greatest potential for success and/or impact on the target market.

2. **To hold**—The objective of this decision is to preserve the current position and/or rank of a training program or intervention. This strategy is used when you believe it is not the proper time to institute a build strategy. The principal focus of this decision is on long-term results, and it is one of the most conservative of the four strategies.

3. **To harvest**—In an attempt to maximize the benefit of training programs or interventions, internal consultants will often use this short-term strategy. It should only be used when training programs or interventions are perceived to have a limited future or acceptance among the target market.

4. **To divest**—This strategy is often used when training programs and interventions have outlived their usefulness. This strategy involves divesting the financial and human resources and assigning them to training programs or in-

terventions that have a greater potential for producing positive results. During periods of economic instability, this approach is used to improve the efficiency of HRD programs and give internal consultants a chance to reduce the number of training programs and interventions offered. This strategy enables you to better use your time and resources.

Cost/benefit analysis.   An important part of a strategic marketing planning process is the creation of a cost/benefit analysis strategy. This strategy demonstrates the relationship between the costs and the benefits of training programs and interventions—a relationship that can serve as a promotional message to be communicated to the decision-makers and upper management.[10]

This strategy begins with naming all potential costs incurred in the design, development, and implementation of training programs and interventions. A second major part of this strategy is identifying benefits received from each training program or intervention. The third phase of this strategy is comparing costs and benefits.

This type of strategy is an excellent way of enhancing and improving the credibility of HRD within the organization. Another positive outcome of this strategy is that it enables you to name the training programs and interventions that produce positive results and those that do not. Then, you can be proactive rather than reactive about the value and importance of training programs and interventions.

Time/location strategy.   Developing a time/location strategy is a very simple, straightforward activity. This strategy should include naming the time, place, and location of all training programs or interventions. When creating a time/location strategy, you should consider the size of the organization, its structure, its geographical dispersion, the number of employees in each given location, the size of the HRD staff, and the financial resources available to the HRD program.

Promotional strategy.   If you do not communicate the value of training programs or interventions to the target market

---

Example of Cost/Benefit Analysis

Mercer's business demands that employees juggle multiple projects, information bases, and client requests every hour of the day. Naturally, time is a valued resource that must be properly managed. In a time management course, participants use a diarylike program to build a job planning system that incorporates long-range objectives, keeps project records, and uses monthly, weekly, and daily plans.

To definitively measure the time and cost savings brought about by the program, we recently surveyed more than 300 Mercer program participants. Responses indicated that, cumulatively, each employee had saved 1.7 hours per week, resulting in enhanced productivity, which can be translated into savings from $500,000 to $750,000 over 1990 and 1991.

---

and decision-makers, no one else in the organization will feel obligated to do so. Therefore, it is essential that you communicate the values and outcomes of HRD. In other words, you must *sell* HRD within the organization.

Selling is not an unprofessional activity. Selling is a way of life. You must realize that you are in a battle for limited human and financial resources of the organization. But to positively impact the organization, you must get a proper share of these resources. And you must be the one who advocates your program. We look at the selling process in greater detail in Chapter 8.

INTEGRATION AND IMPLEMENTATION

The last step in creating a strategic marketing plan is the integration and implementation of each of the five previous steps. You should also consider the three foundational pieces (marketing concept, exchange process, adoption process), which are absolutely critical to successfully developing a strategic marketing plan.

While this step of the strategic marketing planning process may well be self-explanatory, we believe it should be a formal step in the process. It simply consists of reviewing the foundational pieces

FIGURE 7–6
Strategic Marketing Planning Process

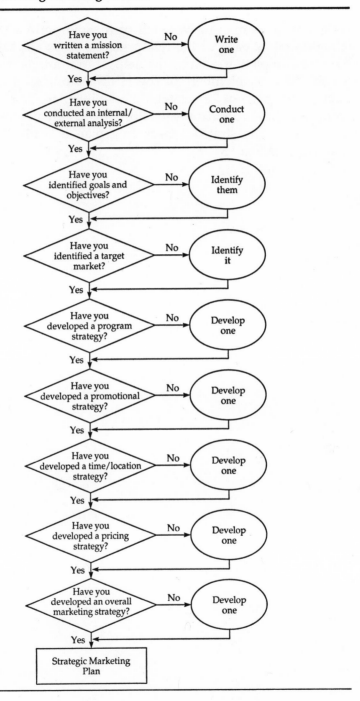

as a way of reminding yourself of their importance. Next, you should look at each of the five previous steps and create a time line for completing each of the steps. Once a time line has been established, all members of the HRD team should discuss and analyze the parts of the strategic marketing plan. This will provide you with a final opportunity to improve and enhance the marketing plan. Then, the strategic marketing plan is ready to be implemented (see Figure 7–6).

Chapter Eight

Using Project Management as a Tool for Internal Consulting

Every internal consultant is a project manager, but not everyone knows how to plan and manage a project. Many project managers lack a practical approach and the techniques for getting a project done efficiently.

WHAT IS A PROJECT?

Perhaps the best way to understand project management is to name the characteristics of a project. Projects vary in size and scope from a simple, one-day training seminar to a comprehensive organizational redesign. A project is an organized effort with planned activities and schedules. It is a one-time effort, and it has specific time-bound results. A project has multiple but interrelated tasks. Finally, a project often involves many people, usually across several functional areas in the organization.

Successful projects consist of several characteristics:

- First, there should be a solid conceptual plan that allows you to produce the desired results. This means the thinking behind the project makes sense and is easily conveyed to others.
- Second, successful projects should contain measurable goals. The goals should be specific, measurable, agreed upon, realistic, and written (see Chapter 6 for more detail).
- Third, successful projects should be broken down into

manageable and clear steps. This process helps you separate large projects into micro projects that are much easier
to manage and control.

- Fourth, each step of a project should be discrete with observable results. Projects are easier to control, and quality
is easier to maintain when observable results have been established.

- Fifth, internal consultants should always have sufficient resources to accomplish the outcomes desired. Resources include financial as well as human.

- Sixth, the team that is assembled to help complete the
project should be focused on the outcomes desired. No
one should question or resist the method of accomplishing
the project or its outcomes.

- Seventh, the resources assembled should be competent
and cooperative. Such resources will ensure higher quality,
promptness, and cost control.

- Finally, successful projects require internal consultants to
constantly check the outcome of the project and give
proper feedback to project team members. To monitor the
outcomes of a project you must identify project controls
before beginning the project.

WHAT IS PROJECT MANAGEMENT?

Project management is a way of thinking; a process of keeping
desired results in focus. Internal consultants, as project managers,
must act to achieve specific objectives within a given budget and
schedule. Project management requires the use of proven tools and
techniques such as critical paths (charts), scheduling technologies
(Gantt charts), goal and risk analysis, stakeholder analysis, and
project networks (these are explained in detail later in this chapter).

Project management involves planning and identifying objectives and activities that produce a desired result. It also includes
organizing people to get the job done and directing them by keeping them focused on achieving the results. Project management
requires internal consultants to measure progress and give feedback to members of the team.

FIGURE 8–1
Project Management Thinking Model

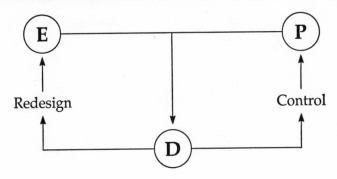

E = Expectations
(milestones, standards, objectives, etc.)

P = Performance
(what's really happening)

D = Discrepancies
(difference between what really happens
and what was expected)

The project management process begins with determining your client's expectations, including specific and expected operations and results (see Figure 8–1). The second part of project management is the systematic measurement of actual progress.

This measurement provides internal consultants with evidence of what is really happening during the project. You can then compare the actual progress to expectations to identify deviations and discrepancies between the two. In other words, you can identify the difference between what really happened and what was expected. This comparison allows you to make decisions that redirect the project and provide corrective actions to narrow the discrepancy between the client's expectations and actual performance.

All projects are bound by a triple constraint: (1) schedules, (2) cost, and (3) quality. Figure 8–2 illustrates this relationship. These triple constraints are much like that of a triangle: a rigid structure, which if changed at any point, dramatically alters its shape.

FIGURE 8–2
The External Triangle

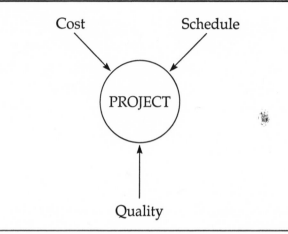

You must identify which of these three constraints is the primary focus of the project. For example, many projects are schedule-focused. In other words, a deadline is driving all of the activities, all of the tasks, and all of the resources. Therefore, decisions are made based on meeting the desired schedule.

As a result, pressure is placed on cost and quality. Often, cost and quality are sacrificed to meet the desired schedule. This thinking is inappropriate for internal consultants, because it does not account for the impact that cost and quality have on the desired result.

Simultaneously, you must guard against allowing projects to be affected by changes in the other two areas during the project. For example, how would having the funding drastically reduced affect the quality and schedule of a project? It would be nearly impossible to produce the same desired results with half the budget or human resources allocated to accomplish it. Therefore, quality of the project will greatly suffer, as will your ability to deliver on time.

TEN MAJOR CAUSES OF PROJECT FAILURE

Internal consultants must constantly guard against project failure. There are several tools and techniques you can use to prevent any of the following from occurring:[1]

1. The project is a solution in search of a problem.
2. Only the project team is interested in the result.
3. No one is in charge.
4. The project plan lacks structure.
5. The project plan lacks detail.
6. The project is underbudgeted.
7. Resources are insufficiently allocated.
8. The project is not tracked against the plan.
9. The project team is not communicating.
10. The project strays from its original goals.

Many of us have worked on projects and have experienced these kinds of problems. How do we prevent them in the future? By planning, organizing, directing, and controlling the project. These activities combine to help you deliver projects on time, within budget, and at a specified level of quality.

PLANNING

Planning involves setting up clear and precise goals and naming work activities that have to take place to carry them out. It includes specific tasks, activities, and expected results. It also includes naming specific dates, times, and people who are responsible for producing the results.

Planning is a prerequisite to control; no plan equals no control. Therefore, before you begin the project, assess the alternatives and identify more than one way to achieve the desired results.

One of the principal outcomes of planning is risk management. This concept is explained in more detail later in the chapter, when we take a look at goal, risk, and stakeholder analysis.

ORGANIZING

Organizing means creating the structure needed to execute the plan. It is a set of activities, responsibilities, and authority relationships needed to execute the plan. Organizing specifies (1) who is responsible for what, (2) who reports to whom, (3) what operations are to be carried out where in the organization, and (4) who is authorized to make which decisions.

In addition to organizing people, project management includes assembling necessary resources (materials and money) to carry out the work defined in the plan. Therefore, organizing incorporates the greatest span of control. Too many activities and people can prevent you from accomplishing the desired results. At the same time, too few of either of these can also produce negative results.

Organizing requires a division of work based on the task and organization's needs, while balancing the authority and responsibility necessary to complete the project. Organizing requires internal consultants to respect the unity of command, which means to name a principal project manager who has the ultimate authority to achieve the desired results.

DIRECTING

Directing involves getting the team to do the project work effectively. It means you communicate with and motivate your team members. Directing is ongoing, not a singular event, often involving coaching, supervision, performance appraisal, and feedback. In certain circumstances, it requires both formal and informal communications. This can include memos, directives, meetings, reports, and informal conversations with team members as needed.

Project managers are much like orchestra conductors. They must constantly know where they are in the plan and give direction to each team member to help them make a contribution to the completion of the project.

CONTROLLING

Once the conceptual plan has been constructed and resources have been assembled, it will be necessary to monitor and keep that structure as the project progresses. You have to compare actual results to planned results and figure out the discrepancies. You must make decisions that are necessary to narrow the gap between expectations and performance.

Therefore, you must have a knowledge of performance (measurement) and a clear and specific understanding of your client's expectations. Often, you have to define and create a proper reporting structure at specific points throughout the project. This report gives you an early warning of discrepancies within the project, and it allows you the time necessary to redesign the project and/or its activities.

Project success depends on early and continuous involvement of you, your staff, and others involved in planning and controlling the project.

THE FIVE PHASES OF PROJECT MANAGEMENT

Project management consists of five phases:

1. Project definition (goal and risk analysis, stakeholder analysis, project network, input, process, output).
2. Scheduling technologies.
3. Budgeting.
4. Project control.
5. Project interfacing, communication, and team leadership.

Each of these phases is critical to carrying out projects that are on time, within budget, and up to the desired quality.

Project Definition

Project definition is based on the belief that a big project is unmanageable, and a small project can be managed. Therefore, big (unmanageable) projects can be broken into a small set of manageable projects. The first task of an internal consultant is to break the project into parts and their respective subparts. This defines the project as a set of interrelated work packages. A *work package* is a group of tasks or activities an individual can complete.

With project definition, you are responsible for managing a series of miniprojects (work packages) rather than managing the entire project. You'll need some tools to accomplish this micro approach to project management:

1. Goal and risk analysis.
2. Stakeholder analysis.
3. Project networks (diagramming and IPO [input, process, and output]).

Each of these tools and techniques makes manageable (micro) projects out of a big (unmanageable) project.

Goal analysis.   Every project has a major goal to be accomplished. The goal is the global statement of purpose and direction that drives all work activities and tasks. The goal serves the following functions:

• Defines the outcome for the product or service.
• Is the continual point of reference for settling disputes and misunderstandings about the project.
• Is the guide that keeps all objectives and other work associated with it on track.
• Enables internal consultants, their customers, and their team to stay focused on the target.
• Creates commitment and agreement about the project outcomes.[2]

Perhaps one of the best ways to capture the project goal is in a statement of the project result: How will we know when we are finished? What will the end result look like?[3]

By approaching project goals in this manner, we are focusing our attention on the users' result. In other words, the client who receives the result of the project is constantly asking the question "What's in it for me?" Therefore, it's critical that you focus your attention on satisfying the end user. Your first step in goal identification is to think about your clients' expectations.

This step requires two-way conversations between you and your clients. You should also talk with the team members assigned to help you carry out the project. Identifying project goals is as much an excuse to develop a dialogue with the end users and project team members as it is to focus your attention on the outcome.

Remember that your goals should meet the criteria discussed in Chapter 6. When you remember this, you will give an adequate focus to the project and create commitment to the result.

FIGURE 8-3
Goal and Risk Analysis

Name of Project: _____

Goal	Measures of Success	Risks
Results the project will achieve and is "accountable" for	How to tell if the goal is achieved	What might go wrong/undesirable results

Figure 8-3 shows how you can identify goals for the project and measurements of success.

Risk Analysis. Also in Figure 8-3 we have supplied space for internal consultants to name the risk associated with carrying out a project's goals. This task makes you think about, "What might go wrong or what undesirable results might occur by accomplishing the project goal?" When completing this section, always consider the three constraints of a project: schedule, cost, and quality.

You should examine what effects limited financial resources will have on completing the project. You should also consider what resources are needed to realistically complete the project and what happens if you can't get those resources promptly. Consider what problems or delays might occur. Look at the impact of these delays on the budget and the overall project schedule and quality.

Consider what the impacts would be of cost overruns or missed deadlines. How will this affect your personal and professional credibility, and what impact will it have on the project?

The answers to all of these questions will help you plan possible backup strategies you may want to use, before you begin the project. By considering the risks of the project before it begins, you can make adjustments to the time line and budget, and get additional resources to proceed in the best possible manner. This process helps you identify the discrepancies between client expectations and actual performance before the project begins, which helps foster better project controls, so you can produce better quality and timely deliverables within the budgets available.

Stakeholder analysis. Stakeholder analysis is another strategic tool internal consultants can use to map and understand planned obligations and tactics when dealing with clients, team members, superiors, and others who stand to gain or lose as a result of a project. The purposes of this analysis are to:

1. Help you identify the groups that must be interacted with to meet project goals.
2. Develop strategies and tactics to effectively negotiate competing goals and interest among the different groups.
3. Identify strategic interest each group has in the project to negotiate common interest.
4. Help internal consultants better allocate resources to deal with these different constituencies to accomplish the project goals.[4]

You may use Figure 8–4 to conduct your stakeholder analysis.

Internal consultants should begin the stakeholder analysis by naming all parties who have something to gain or lose as a result of the project. Next, name the specific interest or expectations you must manage toward. This process will give a baseline for all of your future decision-making and actions. Finally, name the actions you plan to take to meet the interest or expectations of the identified group.

Project networks. Project networks is a tool designed to break large, unmanageable projects into small, manageable ones. It consists of two tools: project diagramming and IPOs (input, process, and output). These tools help you think through a project before you begin.

FIGURE 8–4
Stakeholder Analysis

Stakeholder	Expectation	Action
WHO has a "stake" in the project; who stands to gain or lose?	WHAT is their specific interest or expectation?	WHAT will you have to do to protect their interest and meet their expectation?

Project diagramming. When you begin to think through a project, project diagramming is an excellent tool to use. It helps you think about the major parts of a project and their corresponding subparts. It also allows you to show the relationship between parts and subparts.

Once completed, project diagramming serves as a blueprint or schematic for doing a project. It will help you delegate various project tasks and activities, so the project takes the form of a series of mini projects rather than a large, unmanageable project. It also gives you the opportunity to think about the dependency relationships among parts and subparts before you begin the project.

FIGURE 8–5
Project Diagramming

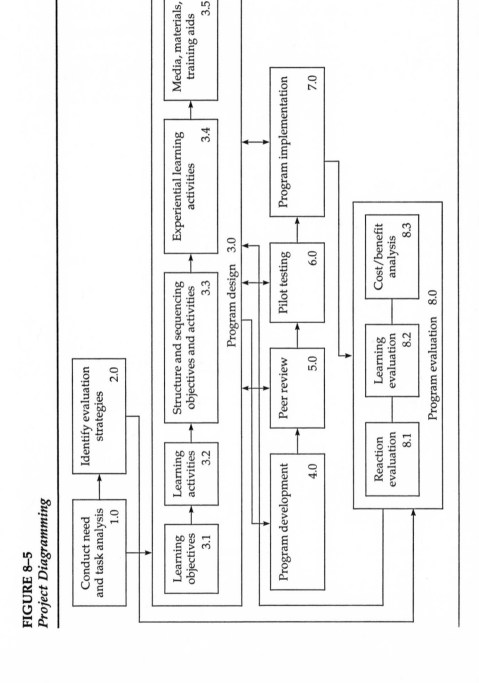

Figure 8–5 is a sample project diagram of a supervisory management training program. This diagram gives an overview of the entire project and its interrelated activities. Each part (1 through 8) represents a major activity and may be divided further (see part 3.0 in Figure 8–5) into subparts. The arrows represent functional dependency, where one part relies on another for one or more of its necessary inputs.

For example, parts 2.0 (Identify evaluation strategies) and 3.0 (Program design) require that part 1.0 (Client's needs assessment) be conducted before engaging in these activities.

Another example of dependency relationships is illustrated when part 5.0 (Peer review), part 6.0 (Pilot testing), part 7.0 (Program implementation) and part 8.0 (Program evaluation) give feedback to a redesign activity, which could occur when each of those parts is complete. In other words, the arrows from parts 5.0, 6.0, 7.0, and 8.0 are directed back to part 3.0, where an internal consultant could engage in a redesign activity based on the feedback received during peer review (5.0), pilot testing (6.0), program implementation (7.0), and program evaluation (8.0).

Part 3 (Program design) is further divided into subparts that can be undertaken during this phase of the project. They include 3.1 (Learning objectives), 3.2 (Learning activities), 3.3 (Structure and sequencing of objectives and activities), 3.4 (Experiential-learning activities) and 3.5 (Media, materials, and training aids). This structure allows internal consultants to diagram a project in greater detail, which helps you identify the resources needed to carry out the project. This also allows you to better communicate with your team members about their responsibilities. Finally, by breaking a project into its subparts, tasks can be easily delegated to team members, which serves as a mini project within the project.

Input, Process, and Output (IPO). Input, Process, and Output (IPO) depicts the detailed operations of a part or subpart. IPO helps you name the inputs (resources) needed to do a part, the process by which it will achieve its outcomes and a list of each intended outcome produced if the process is successful.[5] Inputs, processes, and outputs are designed for each part or subpart of a project (see Figure 8–6).

In combination, project diagramming and IPOs give a complete

FIGURE 8–6
Input, Process, Output (IPO)

Project: _____

Input	Process	Output
Resources needed	Who will do what to obtain results?	What will be the results of successful processes?

picture of a project. They can be used to communicate to clients and project team members the steps for completing a project.

IPOs are the blueprint or schematic for the project. They help break large, unmanageable projects into small, mini projects and allow you to delegate tasks and activities to members of the project team, so they become "mini-project managers." This process greatly enhances the control and management of the project. By using these two tools, you can get your clients and project team members more involved.

Use all of the analyses and tools we have discussed to accurately define your project before it begins. This knowlede will also help you communicate to clients and project team members the desired outcomes and activities of the project. You can make any corrections, additions, or deletions before you allocate expensive and limited financial and human resources. The result is that these four tools will help you better manage projects, so they are within budget, on time, and at desired levels of quality.

Scheduling Technologies

A primary purpose of a project schedule is to name the task dependencies of a project. Another equally important purpose of project scheduling is to identify when resources are most available. Then you can schedule tasks in their proper sequence and allocate resources for maximum efficiency.

A common type of schedule format is a *bar chart* (also called Gantt chart). It is simple to draw, yet it captures a great deal of information about the project plan. It can give a useful overview of the project, and it is a quick management tool for checking project progress.

Bar charts consist of three parts: a time line, a list of activities or tasks, and a bar for each activity (the length of which represents the time estimated for the activity or task). It is often useful to list the project goal at the top of the page.

Figure 8–7 shows how the supervisory management training program previously discussed could be scheduled. Each of the primary work parts is named. Each bar represents the start time of a part (activity or task) and its ending time. The bar chart also represents which task cannot start until other tasks are completed.

A famous saying, "A picture is worth a thousand words" is true for a bar chart. Since bar charts are drawn on one page so you can see an entire project at a glance, they quickly convey a considerable amount of information about the project.

Figure 8–8 shows how resources will be used over time in three different scheduling formats, front-loaded, rear-loaded, and level-loaded schedules.

Front-loaded schedule.   In a front-loaded schedule, most of the resources are consumed and tasks completed in the early

FIGURE 8–7
Typical Training Program Design

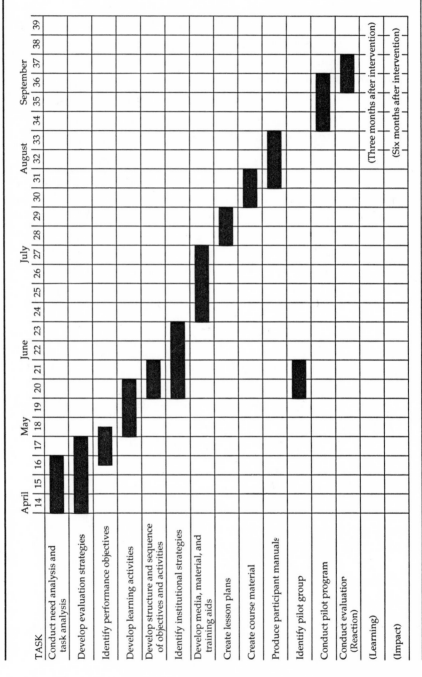

Source: William M. Mercer, Incorporated. Reprinted with permission.

FIGURE 8-8
Three Schedule Formats

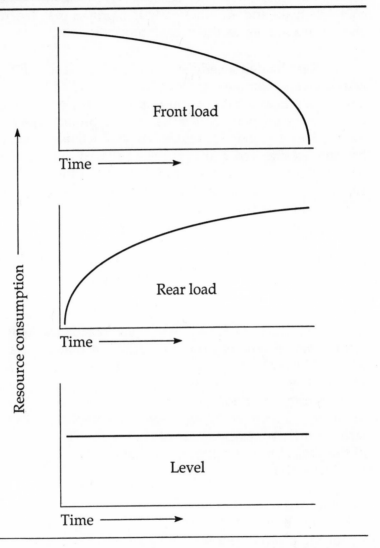

phases of the project. This means you use your resources as early in the project as possible. A risk of front-loaded schedules is that tasks and/or activities are completed so early in the project that the information developed may need to be reviewed later in the project. This schedule often causes project team members to be nervous about doing tasks too early in a project. Another risk associated with front-loaded schedules is that team members who complete tasks and activities early in a project may feel disassociated or abandoned as the project moves forward.

Rear-loaded schedule. In a rear-loaded schedule, you use resources and complete tasks at the very end of the project time line. This schedule allows you to prepare project team members for an increasing workload at the end of a project. The risk associated with a rear-loaded schedule is that all activities and tasks must be carefully checked and time lines adhered to for the project to be completed on time, because there is no time at the end for slippage.

This schedule can create a stressful situation for project team members and cause slippage in the quality of the project. In addition, cost overruns are most common with this type of schedule because project managers have not allocated enough resources, and therefore, must acquire additional ones to meet the project deadline.

Level-loaded schedule. A level-loaded schedule is the most common type of project schedule. It may not be the most practical or realistic type of schedule but it is indeed frequently used to demonstrate scheduling technologies. This type of schedule uses resources and completes tasks equally from the beginning to the end of a project. It allows you to complete tasks in a linear fashion, in that one resource could be assigned to complete all tasks of the project from beginning to end.

With front- and rear-loaded schedules, you may need to allocate multiple resources to carry out multiple tasks at the same time. Level-loaded schedules are the most common, but they are often unrealistic. If managed correctly, however, they provide continuity for the project from beginning to end.

Scheduling constraints. On the surface, scheduling seems relatively simple. Some constraints, however, make the process difficult, and often lead to less-than-ideal schedules such as:

1. The availability of particular resources during the project.

2. Demands on resource needs for other present or future projects.

3. Different or conflicting demands by internal consultants for some resources.

4. A desire to avoid extensive work overloads for particular individuals.

5. Available resources to do a particular task.

6. Budgetary constraints.

7. Desire to cut write-offs or budget overruns.

8. Integration and use of other project targets using the same resources.

9. A reasonable time for doing activities that are uncertain.

10. Technical constraints that may need extra time.

11. Difficulties inherent in scheduling far in advance.

Many, if not all of these constraints, can prevent you from producing projects on time, within budget, and up to quality standards.

Budgeting

When developing a budget, you must consider all costs of completing a project. To maximize control, you should begin building budgets at the component level of the project, so the budget is linked to a part and its subparts. Then, you can examine budgetary costs at a micro level within the project rather than at a macro level.

When building a budget, internal consultants should consider five different types of costs:

1. Direct costs.

2. Indirect costs.

3. Fixed costs.

4. Variable costs.

5. Allocated costs.

You should name each of these costs for *every* part and subpart of the project. That way, you can build a project budget from the inside out rather than identifying a budget in an arbitrary and inconsistent manner.

Direct costs.   Direct costs are all items that can be directly attributed to the project, part or subpart. These costs include equipment, time, travel, supplies, tools, and dedicated human resources to the project. These costs often require actual dollars rather than portions of your annual budget.

Indirect costs.   Indirect costs are items that are difficult to attribute to specific projects, parts or subparts. They include such arbitrary items as heating, electricity, insurance, and other overhead expenses. They should be accounted for as a percentage of the overall budget of a given fiscal period rather than allocated to each project, part, or subpart. It is important to remember that these costs will be expended whether or not you engage in 1, 10, or 100 projects. These are the costs most often overlooked by internal consultants when building project budgets.

Fixed costs.   Fixed costs are those that do not vary according to how much they are used. They are, therefore, predictable. An example would be allocation of rent expense, computer equipment, and certain types of human resources (e.g., secretaries and administrative assistants). These items can be used as often or as much as you need them without greatly affecting the overall project budget.

Variable costs.   Variable costs are items that vary with their usage. They are often hard to predict and control. They can include such things as long-distance telephone calls, copying and other disposable materials, mainframe computer costs, and outside consultant expenses.

Remember that variable costs often need special control efforts to keep them to a minimum, because they can get out of hand unless you watch project expenses closely. These types of costs lead to cost overruns more than do any others.

Allocated costs.   Allocated costs for human resources and other items already "paid for" by the organization are in this classification. The most common types of costs in this category are the salaries and benefits of secretaries, administrative assistants, receptionists, and other office personnel. If they are to be assigned to a given project, part or subpart, they should be estimated by proportions of use (e.g., numbers of hours for human resources) versus an actual dollar amount.

In other words, if an administrative assistant is assigned to the project, you should identify the percentage of time that is spent on the project in relation to 100 percent of their allocated time. Then, you can request, for example, one fourth of an administrative assistant's time during a year for a given project. This request is easier to communicate to superiors than a dollar amount.

Project Controls

Project controls help you successfully complete a project by comparing actual progress against plans. Controls enable you to compare your performance against your clients' expectations. Then, you can make adjustments to cut discrepancies between performance and expectations.

Project controls focus on one or more of the three major parts of a project: time, costs, or quality standards. There are three reasons for using project controls. They are (1) to track progress, (2) to detect variances from the plan, and (3) to take corrective action.

To track progress.   Use project controls to check the progress of parts and subparts. This is important because of the interdependency of tasks and activities during the project. Failure to carry out certain tasks may ultimately jeopardize the time line, budget, and quality of the project. Therefore, it is critically important to check the status of every activity in a project.

To detect variance from plan.   Early in this chapter, we discussed the importance of identifying client expectations compared to actual performance during a project. This process helps cut the discrepancies between the expectations and performance so you can make adjustments and take corrective actions as necessary.

To take corrective action.   If you are tracking the progress of parts and subparts to find the discrepancy between expectations and performance, you can find out whether or not corrective action is needed, and then act appropriately. When problems occur, projects fall behind schedule, exceed budget, and jeopardize quality. For this reason, you must make decisions that enable the project to get back on schedule. This decision may require reallocating human and financial resources, adjusting time lines, and reducing client expectations.

Types of Controls

There are three types of controls you can use to make certain projects remain on track. They include: (1) steering controls, (2) go-no-go controls, and (3) postaction controls.

Steering control. When a project reaches a critical checkpoint, internal consultants compare the current status of the project with the desired status. If the activities and tasks don't meet your expectations, you carry out a set of corrective actions known as *steering controls.* Steering controls redirect and steer tasks to help internal consultants adhere to the project plan. They are used to answer the question, *if/then,* and are most useful when you have to make critical decisions at key points in the project. Steering controls should be named before the project begins and serve as a checkpoint during the project.

Go-no-go control. A go-no-go control is similar to a steering control, but the corrective action is different. For example, if a project reaches a critical checkpoint and doesn't meet the status requirements desired, you stop the project. This control limits the use of costly financial and human resources, and allows them to be reallocated to projects that have a higher potential for success.

Postaction controls. Finally, postaction controls allow you and project team members to discuss how the project was managed after it is complete and the successes and failures of the project. This control gives you feedback from project team members about their perspective of how the project progressed, and it allows you to give feedback to members of the project team about their performance and ways of improving it.

Project controls are most effective when projects consist of tasks and activities that have a high-dependency relationship to stay on

FIGURE 8–9
Type of Control and Control Point Worksheet

Type of control	Critical function	Hard to manage	Plan uncertain	"Public eye"
Steer to guide toward objective				
Check to decide "go-no-go" (yes-no control)				
Post-action control for file or reporting				

schedule. In addition, projects that are hard to manage are also excellent candidates for project controls. Also, when a project has never been conducted before, project planning is uncertain. Therefore, you should use project controls more freely.

Last, projects that are very important to senior management and other critical decision-makers should include project controls because these projects are in the public eye. Figure 8–9 is a worksheet that you can use to name the types of control by control point.

Regardless of the type of project controls used or the conditions under which they are used, they are important tools to make sure projects are completed on time, within budget, and up to quality standards.

Project Interfacing, Communication, and Leadership

Internal consultants must develop excellent communication and leadership skills for project management to be successful. You must clearly and specifically define each project team member's role and responsibilities, define their expectations for performance, and communicate performance criteria so project team members can evaluate their own performance. This process will allow project team members to take corrective action rather than having to wait for you to notice discrepancies in performance. Internal consultants should also allow project team members to suggest ways of improving performance.

Clearly communicate the project goals and purposes to empower project team members and help them become more committed to the project's success. Also, involve team members in developing a project definition. This includes goal and risk analysis, stakeholder analysis, project diagrams, and IPO analysis. Complete a stakeholder analysis on each project team member and communicate the results to them. Then, allow time for project team members to respond about their expectations and interests in the success of the project.

Always conduct a project kickoff meeting and go over the project, its parts, subparts, and work assignments, and develop a communication plan (Figure 8-10). A communication plan includes who will report on what and when, when meetings will be held, and how meetings will be conducted. During the kickoff meeting, you should discuss the project team members' responsibilities and roles.

Communicate how project team members will be rated and set up communication vehicles for the project.

Set up and keep a "no surprise" atmosphere. Make it clear that you expect to be notified early of problems. Tell them that honesty is never punished and that team members will be rewarded and supported for keeping you informed. Also stress that project team members are responsible for identifying solutions to problems during the project. And communicate that you expect project team members to supply feedback throughout the project.

TWELVE GUIDES FOR EFFECTIVE PROJECT LEADERSHIP

To manage a project effectively, you must adopt a leadership style that both motivates and empowers project team members, and monitors and guides their progress.[6] Use the following guidelines to do this:[7]

FIGURE 8–10
Communication Planning Worksheet

Stakeholders	Information Needed	Communication Method
With whom must you communicate?	What kinds of information do they need?	How will you keep them informed?

PEOPLE REQUIRING COMMUNICATION LINKAGES: All stakeholders—team members, contractors, customers, bosses, production coordinators, and so forth.

KINDS OF INFORMATION NEEDS: Status reports, approval of goals, approval for activities and resources, inspections, review of plans, approval to involve staff, feedback on team-member performance, expenditure data, brief updates, notification of meetings, evaluation data, and so forth.

COMMUNICATION ACTIVITIES: Team meetings, management briefings, memos, progress reports, "newsletters," formal reports, exception reports, informal meetings, sign-off and approval forms, and so forth.

1. Do not over-direct, over-observe, or over-report.
2. Recognize differences in individuals. Have a keen appreciation for each person's unique characteristics.
3. Help subordinates see problems as changes.
4. Assess your employees about ways they think they are more creative or would like to be more creative, and what sort of creative contributions they would like most to make.

5. Allow more freedom for individuals to guide their own work.

6. Train yourself and others to respond to the positive parts of proposed ideas rather than react to often easy-to-spot negative ones.

7. Develop greater frustration tolerance for mistakes and errors.

8. Provide a safe atmosphere for failure.

9. Be a resource person rather than a controller; a helper rather then a boss.

10. Be a buffer between employees and outside problems or "higher-up demands."

11. Enhance your own creative ability through special workshops and seminars, specialized readings, and creative exercises and games.

12. Make sure that innovative ideas are sent to your boss with your support and backing; then insist on a feedback mechanism. Without feedback, the flow of creative ideas dries up because innovators feel their ideas are not given a fair hearing or taken seriously.

EVOLUTION OF A PROJECT TEAM

Newly formed project teams go through a developmental cycle or stages:[8]

1. Forming stage.
2. Storming stage.
3. Norming stage.
4. Performing stage.

Forming Stage

During the forming stage, project team members are getting acquainted and starting to build relationships. They are trying to decide what types of behavior will be accepted, what the team task is, and how the group will go about carrying out its work. It is a period of orientation and dependency, and project team members look to leaders for guidance and leadership.

Storming Stage

The storming stage is a period of conflict among project team members and resistance to the task. This phase is characterized by a hostility among team members and toward the leaders as members resist the structure of the group. It is during this stage that team members test each other and develop a sense of boundaries and trust. Internal consultants should expect conflict during this stage.

Norming Stage

A sense of group cohesion develops. The acceptance of unwritten codes of conduct and behavior are developed and shared. There is an increased willingness to make the project work and information is freely shared and acted on. It is a period of openness and trust among project team members.

Performing Stage

The final stage in the evolution of a project team is the performing stage. During this phase, interpersonal relationships have stabilized, the roles are clarified and the team moves toward producing the desired result. The group is clearly defined and structure, purpose, and individual roles are further clarified. The emphasis during this phase is on results, so there is considerable problem-solving and decision-making.

By identifying the evolutionary stage of a project team, you are in a better position to adjust to the concerns of the group. Remember, the goal is to become and keep a high-performing team. Internal consultants must use their communication skills, understanding of group cohesion, conflict resolution skills, and coaching skills to allow the group to reach the performing stage.

Treat each member of the project team with respect and dignity. Always listen to the points of view and perspectives of each team member, and allow them to express their thoughts and feelings freely. Withhold judgment until you completely understand the circumstances, events, and factors affecting the team member's point of view or perspective.

Project Management Model

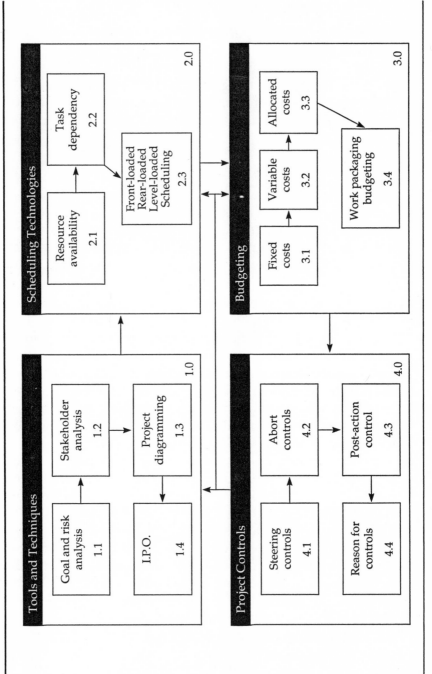

Chapter Nine

Managing the Client Relationship

ESTABLISHING RAPPORT: OVERCOMING "NO TRUST"

Internal consultants must learn that clients do not become "clients" unless they trust that *you* can help them look good in the organization. This may include improving their performance, their employees' performance, their supervisory/management skills, their communication skills, and so forth.

People buy from people. Regardless of how much the HRD program may help your clients look good in the organization, clients will not buy into your program unless they trust **you.**

Gaining your clients' trust takes more than being "trustworthy." It involves five steps.

1. Establishing commonality and empathy with the client.
2. Maintaining credibility in everything you do.
3. Defining your intentions or reasons for your actions and how those actions can help your client.
4. Being responsive to your clients' needs, goals, and objectives, whether personal or organizational.
5. Being accountable for your actions and for the results of the HRD program you are "selling."

Establishing Commonality and Empathy with the Client

People buy what they are comfortable with; what they know. It is important to find a level of commonality with your clients, if you are going to be successful.

Commonality doesn't mean you have to be exactly like the client. It means you need to have an understanding of what they need and value and empathy for where they are coming from and for what they are hoping to accomplish.

Charles Butters, director of organizational planning at LTV Corporation, said that to achieve commonality means you will have to understand the performance deficiencies, organizational pressures, budget constraints, sales goals, supervisory problems, and/or employee dissatisfaction your client may be facing before you can help them decide on an HRD solution.

The concept of commonality is similar to the phrase, "walk a mile in their shoes." If you can show that you understand the client's problem and goals, and you share their concern for reaching those goals, you will be a successful internal consultant.

For example, if your client wants to improve the teamwork of the work unit, and you decide that a team-building course would be beneficial, you first must prove several things before the client is likely to buy into your team-building program:

1. You understand why the group is not working as a team, and have suggested solutions for correcting the problem.
2. You understand that improving the team's performance is critical to improving the unit's bottom line.
3. You understand that the group must continue to get the work done; they cannot devote several work days to a team-building program.
4. The team-building program can be tailored to meet the characteristics of this particular group; a team-building program for manufacturing workers will be very different from a program for software engineers.
5. You have conducted successful team-building programs for similar groups of employees.

Once you have discussed these items of commonality with your client, the client will see that you indeed have a good grasp of the situation, understand the objectives, and can provide a solution to the problem. That's the first step in managing the client relationship.

Maintaining Credibility in Everything You Do

Credibility is an internal consultant's lifeblood. If your clients do not perceive you as being credible, you will never gain their trust.

One important factor in credibility is to "do what you say you're going to do." If you commit to conducting an HRD program on a given date that will deliver certain results, you had better follow through on that date with a program that delivers those results. If you don't, your client may not give you another chance. And once a client is lost, they are usually lost forever.

Another factor in credibility relates to commonality, discussed previously. As an internal consultant, you must show that you not only have knowledge in the HRD field, but also that you can **adapt your knowledge** to your client's business or industry. When you can take generic information and tailor it to meet your client's specific needs, you gain credibility with your audience.

For example, if you are teaching a sales training course to a group of personal computer salespeople at Apple Corporation, you would focus on the fundamentals of selling a "product," and a high-end, sophisticated product at that. On the other hand, if you were teaching the same course to a group of consultants, you would focus on the art of selling a "service."

Your broad knowledge of sales techniques would apply to both groups, but your focus would need to be entirely different for the two groups. The way you present the material, the emphasis on the content, and the examples and applications you use would be very different for the two groups. If you were not able to tailor the course to match "what the participants know," the course would appear irrelevant, and you would lose credibility with your audience.

As an example of the *opposite* approach, a person who **unsuccessfully** attempted to be an internal consultant in a large consulting organization was teaching a course on time management. He was teaching the course to a group of senior consultants, who sell nothing but their expertise and time to clients. The internal consultant told this group that they would be better able to manage their workday if they would return client phone calls during a two-hour period only, ignoring client calls all other times.

Obviously, the consultants in the room were appalled, thinking about their clients who expect responsiveness and ultimate commitment. Needless to say, the internal consultant was not successful in that organization.

Finally, credible internal consultants must "know their stuff." Before you offer an HRD program, you had better be fully knowledgeable about the subject. If you are not, your class will spot it and the game is over. That does not mean you can't say you will find out more information on a topic and get back to the class or individual. No one is expected to know everything off the top of their head. But you better know most of the answers expected of you, or you will lose credibility with your group.

Defining Your Intent

Another important step in managing the client relationship is to have your client "buy into" the solution. You can do this by getting your client involved in developing the solution from the beginning.

When you know you have a solution to an HRD problem, you should discuss your proposed actions with the client to explain why you believe your approach is the best one. Then, see what the client's reaction is to your program. Perhaps the client will think of some alternatives that are better suited to the organization's employees or consider the pertinent environmental factors going on in the organization at the time. The insights that sometimes only the client can give will improve your HRD program and give the client some ownership in the solution.

On the other hand, if you do not explain your intentions or actions and merely proceed down **your** chosen path, you may be blindsided by your client's reaction. In the end, that could hurt your career, your credibility, and the desired results of the HRD program.

You probably will have one of two types of clients. Judy Campbell, president of Campbell & Associates, believes some clients like to be heavily involved in every phase of the program, from setting goals and objectives, to reviewing the course material, to taking part in the program itself. These clients may be more difficult to deal with along the way, but they have a lot of ownership in the program and will be "champions" of the HRD program internally.

She believes other clients will leave those decisions to you and will expect you to deliver the expected results. Since this type of client does not have any ownership in the program, they are usually much more difficult to please and will likely judge you and the program's results much tougher. When you deliver the results they expect, however, they will continue to trust you and give you complete autonomy.

You can establish a trusting relationship with either type of client; a relationship where the client will turn to you for all of the organization's HRD needs. That is the ultimate compliment from a client. You want them to count on you for everything related to your field.

Being Responsive to Your Clients' Needs, Goals, and Objectives

You can have all of the credibility, knowledge, and respect in the world, but if you don't respond to your clients' needs, you will lose them.

Responsiveness is an important attribute of managing the client relationship. The reason clients turn to you for support and service is they can count on you to deliver. When they can count on you, they will continue to "rehire" you. But if they can't count on you, they'll go to someone else.

To be successful, you must be responsive in several areas:

- **Needs, goals, and objectives**—This area of responsiveness in the client relationship is most important, so it is critical that you understand what the needs, goals and objectives are, and then make sure the HRD program meets them.

  For example, if your client wants employees to deliver better client service by becoming better project managers, your project management course better include techniques for improving client service. If the course only focused on managing the project schedule and budget, you would not meet your client's needs, goals, and objectives in this instance.

- **Timetable**—If the client has a deadline for achieving certain goals or milestones, you must deliver an HRD program that will help the client meet that time frame. Or if the client's employees are only available for your program during a given time, you may have to adjust your schedule to accommodate their availability. That adjustment might mean moving up a course that isn't quite ready or delaying a course you are anxious to teach.

- **Budget**—A budget includes both money and time. If HRD programs in your organization are charged back to the division using the program, you will have to work within your client's training budget to deliver the necessary programs within the budget. However, if HRD is not charged back to the client, you still have to consider the budget of "time." Few clients will allow their employees to attend many training sessions in a year. More likely, you will have the client's employees for short periods and for only a few times each year. So you've got to make the most of the time you have with the audience.

- **Image and reputation within the organization**—Clients who are champions of HRD will continue to champion the cause as long as it does not harm their image and reputation inside the organization, according to Ron Walker, executive vice president of William M. Mercer, Incorporated. If your client is receiving the desired results from the HRD programs you're providing, the client will "have something to show for it." This will make your client look smart for using your program.

  The opposite, however, can also be true. If your client's image is tainted because he is supporting an HRD program that doesn't deliver, he will almost certainly back away from being a champion.

- **Other departments within the organization, if necessary**— Usually in the consulting relationship, you end up having more than one "client" in an organization, and you have to please all of them.

  For example, your primary client may be the director of human resources. This person believes in your programs, believes in you, and believes in the need for HRD in the organization. However, to carry out the HRD programs effectively, you will likely have to also convince, or sell, the director of other departments such as operations, finance, systems, and so forth. That's because the employees of those departments may be your audience, so you need the support of their director.

  The human resources director may have some influence

on employees' participation, but ultimately, line management has responsibility for budgets, schedules, and its employees' time.

Being Accountable for Your Actions

Any good consulting arrangement includes a means of measuring success, which is how your clients hold you accountable for your actions.

When you begin planning the HRD program to meet your client's needs, goals, and objectives, you should also build in a measurement mechanism. This could include follow-up statistical measurements compared to benchmark measurements, gathering employee and management opinions about "perceived" improvement, or physically measuring attainment of targets or milestones.

Once you can point to concrete evidence that proves the success of your program, you foster credibility and gain momentum for additional training throughout the organization.

THE CLIENT MANAGEMENT SKILLS YOU WILL NEED

Judging from the steps previously described, it should be clear that client management is hard work. To be successful, you need a variety of consulting skills, including:

1. Interpersonal skills.
   (*a*) Listening.
   (*b*) Questioning.
   (*c*) Communication.
   (*d*) Feedback.
   (*e*) Negotiation.
2. Presentation skills.

These skills are interrelated in consulting and client management. You can be partially successful if you have only some of the skills. But you can successfully manage your client relationships if you have **all** of these consulting skills.

Interpersonal Skills

Listening.   The art of listening goes far beyond "hearing" what your client says. Listening requires that you not only hear the **words,** but also the **tone** in which they are said and the words that are **not said.**

Often, it is the tone of the words that truly conveys the meaning. For example, try repeating this sentence, each time putting the emphasis on a different word:

"*I* didn't say he was a bad consultant."

"I *didn't* say he was a bad consultant."

"I didn't *say* he was a bad consultant."

"I didn't say *he* was a bad consultant."

"I didn't say he *was* a bad consultant."

"I didn't say he was a *bad* consultant."

"I didn't say he was a bad *consultant.*"

Although the words are exactly the same in each sentence, the *meaning* is different for each, simply because the emphasis or tone is different for each one. The successful internal consultant will learn to listen for hidden meaning by listening to the nuances of *tone.*

In addition to listening for tone, you should also listen for what your client is *not* saying. Successful internal consultants listen for what is not being said to try to decide the *real* problem.

As an example, if your client is telling you that his engineering staff has low morale and needs team-building training, you could take that at face value and offer a team-building course. After the course, however, the engineers may not show anymore "team" characteristics or improved morale than they showed before they took the course.

The reason is because the *real* problem is that the engineers are overworked because they do not know how to manage their time or their projects. Therefore, they are working long hours without "catching up," which is contributing to the low morale.

Instead of a team-building course, these people need time management and project management training. But if you don't ask the right questions and probe into what you are hearing, you may never uncover the real problem. And you can't possibly offer the correct solution.

Questioning. Listening leads to the next critical client management skill: questioning. This skill is as important as listening because they go hand-in-hand.

A good internal consultant asks all kinds of questions about all kinds of topics to get as much information as possible. Your clients may even wonder why you're asking some of the questions you're asking. But it's important to cover every angle of the conversation with questions if you're going to get all of the information.

There are six types of questions you may want to consider using:

1. **Open-end probes:** These questions give clients an opportunity to say anything, from a terse, clipped phrase to a rambling dissertation. Answers can be encouraging, discouraging, or neutral. For example, "What is the most logical next step?"

2. **Closed questions:** These questions seek a very limited response, like yes or no. Sometimes these questions are necessary, but using too many of them can annoy the person and may cause you to miss out on some critical information. For example, "Should we schedule a pilot course at your office?"

3. **Pauses:** Short silences are also probes. A pause is an intentional period of silence designed to create involvement with the client.

4. **Reflective statements:** These statements mirror the behavior you are observing; they are empathetic statements that show you care. For example, "You seem hesitant . . ."

5. **Summary statements:** These statements recap what you've learned from the other person. They reword the client's ideas and remarks. For example, "So you're pleased with the quality of the course, but you would like to move up the schedule."

6. **Best-least:** Best-least probes are questions that help you understand other potential opportunities in a client situation by uncovering additional information. For example, "What do you like best about the course? What do you like least?"

Some typical questions you may want to use during your client discussions are:

- What are you trying to accomplish?
- What behaviors are you trying to change, or what performance are you trying to improve?
- Who should be involved in the HRD program, and why?
- What do you expect the results of the HRD program to be?
- What do you think your employees will expect from the HRD program?
- When would be the best time to conduct the training program? Why?
- What is the best location for the training program?
- How do you want to measure the results of the program?
- What will be the follow-up activity? How often?

Communication.   Once you have gathered all of the information through listening and questioning, you will need to communicate with your client about the course of action that will best meet your client's needs. Oliver London, area vice president of organizational effectiveness at Brown & Forman, Inc., recently told us that it doesn't do any good to know the solution to the problem if you can't sufficiently communicate it to your client.

Communication happens between two or more people. One person alone cannot "communicate." That's because communication is *encoding* the message (saying the words), filtering the "noise" (distractions and biases), and *decoding* the message (listening to the words). Without all three steps, you do not have communication.

It's not enough to tell your clients what you want them to hear. Before your client "hears" your message, clients will first filter it through a thought process, organizational "distractions" (other people's opinions, etc.) and personal biases. Then, clients will decide what it is they "heard." And what they heard is not always what you "said." That's where communication can break down.

To avoid that problem:

- Always clarify with your clients what *you* heard them say.
- Repeat back to them what the next steps will be for you and for them.
- Document the conversation, including purpose, goals/objectives, suggested solutions, schedules, and if applicable, budgets.
- Get agreement from your clients that that was, in fact, what they understood, as well.

Then continue to communicate with your clients. Keep clients informed of your progress, how well you're adhering to the schedule, any problems you are having and how you're correcting them, and any action you want them to take to move the process along.

Always get their agreement before you move on to the next major step, which includes reviewing preliminary course outlines and materials with your clients before you actually conduct the training course so there is time to change the content, if necessary. This exchange also gives your clients a stake in the outcome.

Feedback. The successful internal consultant will give **and** receive feedback on the HRD program.

Giving feedback comes into play when you are discussing the situation with your client and designing the solution. During these times, you will want to give your clients feedback about their interpretation of what the problem is and their expectations for solving the problem. Their assessment may not be realistic or accurate, as you read the situation. Therefore, having a dialogue—giving and receiving information—will help to make sure you and your client are on the same track.

Receiving feedback is very important to your continued success in the organization. It is the only way you will know how well you're meeting your clients' needs and the needs and expectations of their employees.

You should ask for feedback at several points and from various people:

- During your initial "problem definition" discussions with your clients; feedback comes from your client and others in the organization who are involved in defining the problem.
- While you are designing the course content and materials to solve the problem; feedback comes from your client and, perhaps, from a few course participants.
- During the course itself; feedback comes from the participants.
- After the course; feedback comes from participants—in the way of an evaluation—and also comes from your client. Your client will have feedback either because he attended the session or because he received feedback from the participants. This latter feedback may be more "real" than the feedback participants are willing to give you directly.

Negotiation. Webster's dictionary defines *negotiation* as: "to confer, bargain, or discuss, with a view to reaching an agreement." Negotiation is a give-and-take process, ending in some type of agreement by both parties.

When negotiating, avoid taking a position. If you take a position, you're no longer open to a negotiation. Instead, try to focus on the interests of both parties. Consider the alternatives and options available to each; discuss those and the advantages and disadvantages of each.

Consider how legitimate the other party's proposal might be: Is it realistic? Can you live with their idea, if that is the negotiated position? Finally, get a commitment from both sides to live up to the negotiated position.

Sometimes, you may have to negotiate with your clients to steer the process in the direction you know is best. For example, let's say your client wants you to offer a certain training course by a given date because that is when the employees are available. However, you know the course will not be ready by that date. What you have to do is either negotiate a different date with your client or risk the credibility and integrity of the course by offering it before it is ready.

If you do not successfully negotiate a different date, the course may fail, which will hurt the credibility of the entire HRD program and will not meet your client's needs. Then, you run the risk of having your client doubt your ability to improve performance in the organization.

If you negotiate a later date, however, you have a much greater chance of presenting a successful course and meeting your clients' needs. Clients may not like having to move the date back, but when they see the results, they will be glad they waited.

Presentation Skills

Skills in public speaking and organizing your thoughts into a concise presentation are invaluable to internal consultants. When you are training, you use presentation skills all the time. But you also need to know how to present your ideas and concepts outside of the classroom.

Internal consultants are brought in early from the top of the organization when decisions need to be made about organizational change and performance modification, because internal consultants truly "consult" on what should be done; they do not merely take orders about the programs to offer. Because of this high-level contact, you must be able to articulate your ideas to senior management clearly, concisely, and quickly.

KEEPING YOUR CLIENTS HAPPY

The ultimate goal of "managing the client relationship" is to keep your clients happy with your performance.

Educate the Client

One reason your clients turn to you as an internal consultant is they value your expertise. You provide knowledge and skills they do not have. It will be helpful to you in the long term, however, if you educate your clients about HRD and the training courses you offer. Because the more the clients know about your business, the more they will appreciate it and you. Also, all clients like to think they know something about what their consultants do, or else they wouldn't feel confident monitoring the consultant's performance. So help your clients feel more fulfilled by teaching them more about what you do.

Turn Your Assertions into Questions

There is nothing worse than an internal consultant "telling the client what to do." You must get the clients involved by asking for their opinion, asking what they prefer; make your clients feel like the ideas are their ideas. We've heard several organizational leaders say that there is nothing they hate more than having a consultant tell them what to do instead of asking what they think about a recommendation. The consultant probably knows more than does the client in their respective field, but the consultant should never assume that the client doesn't have an opinion or is going to blindly follow along with everything the consultant suggests.

Give Clients Options

This concept goes hand-in-hand with the previous item. Whenever possible, give your clients alternatives to choose from rather than telling them that "it's best to go this way only." Clients much prefer to weigh the alternatives and ask for your recommendation than to be told that they better do something a certain way. Remember, they are the boss. Many of them pay the bills. Unless they are compromising your integrity or heading down a path you know is doomed, let them have some freedom in the decision. They'll grow to respect **your** opinions that way.

Make Meetings, Reports, and Materials Meaningful

No one has time to waste, least of all your clients. When meeting with them, be prepared with an agenda and stay within the allotted time frame. Cover all of the salient points first, and then hit on less important points if time allows. Make your reports and course materials as concise and easy-to-read as possible. If practical, include an executive summary of the pertinent information in the front of reports and course summaries. Your client may spend time reading that section only and may rely on you to fill him in on the rest of the content.

Help Your Client Use What You Deliver

Once the training course or HRD program is complete, make it easy for your clients to continue using the skills everyday by supplying follow-up activities, refresher courses, performance measurement techniques, focus groups, incentives to continue using the skills, and so forth. No matter how good a training program is, it is useless if your audience does not remember to use the new skills once they have walked out of the room. You then have only given information, you have not changed behavior.

Be Accessible

Be sure your clients know they can reach you when they want to. If you're not available at once, be sure someone knows how to contact you, so you can get back to your client. Return telephone calls as soon as you can. Respond to questions quickly with as much information as you can. If your clients are spread across the country, you may have to fly to their locations several times each month just to be where you're needed. But if it keeps your clients happy and they keep "hiring" you, you've accomplished your objectives.

Give Away Some Freebies

Everyone likes to get something for nothing. Let your clients do the same. Your clients will appreciate it if you can offer them a free course, or sit down with their management team and help them set goals and objectives for their departments, or provide free follow-up monitoring after a program.

Audit Your Service Quality

You should constantly be getting feedback from your clients on how well you're doing. This kind of feedback isn't merely an evaluation after a training course. What we're talking about here is a face-to-face meeting with your clients to find out how well they think you're delivering what they need. Ask them open-ended questions that they have to think about, such as "What performance improvements have you noticed in your employees over the past six months?" "How do you think that improvement is attributable, or not attributable, to our HRD program?" "What are the three best things that have come out of the HRD program for you and your employees?" "What are three things we can still improve?"

Also, at least once a year, your supervisor should meet with your clients to find out how well they think you're doing.

Always, Always Add Value

Any HRD professional can stand up in front of a class and teach a course. However, internal consultants add value because they are able to help the client sort out problem "symptoms" from problem "causes," offer **unique** ways of solving those problems, and give the client more than he expected.

You can decide if you're adding value or not by answering this question, "Can my client do this without me?" If the answer is yes, chances are you are not adding real value for your client. He may not realize it yet, but he will if that behavior continues. If your client cannot acquire that skill set or solve that problem without you, however, you are providing services that are of real value to your client.

Adding value is a continuous process. After you have added value in one area for awhile, the client may no longer perceive that as value-added service because he'll come to expect it. It is important that you continually find new areas and ways to add value. Try to stay one step ahead of your client's thinking curve by continually offering suggestions and new ideas he hasn't thought of. You may even help him discover a need he didn't know he had. When you do, and you can meet that need, you have truly become an internal consultant.

Chapter Ten

Improving Organizational Effectiveness through the Problem-Solving Process

To improve organizational effectiveness, internal consultants should help managers and supervisors **increase productivity and efficiency** through the problem-solving process. This process allows you to use your problem-solving, interpersonal, and consulting skills. It also enhances your credibility and image among organizational leaders when you help them solve problems.

THE PROBLEM-SOLVING PROCESS

Expectation/Performance Identification

The problem-solving process begins with identifying expectations (i.e., production, service, marketing) of executives, managers, and supervisors and comparing them to actual performance. Management expectations are the "desired state," conditions, or circumstances that management prefers. "Performance" is the realistic outcome or behaviors that presently exist in the organization.

Problem Identification

Analyze the situation to identify expectations and determine the current situation. The discrepancy between these two positions is the "problem(s)" facing the organization. The focus of the problem-solving process is finding the "best" solution to the problem(s). During this phase, you help management identify proper actions designed to close the gap between expectations and actual performance.

Solution Identification

Brainstorm with others to generate as many ideas as possible to identify a solution. This activity should be conducted without evaluating or examining the ideas. The goal is to come up with as many potential solutions as possible.

Solution Analysis

Once all of the possible solutions have been identified, you and management can analyze each one. Set up criteria to serve as a standard or benchmark by which to filter each idea. Ideas that meet most of the criteria are grouped together for further analysis. The ideas that don't meet the established criteria should be filed for future consideration.

Solution Selection

Test the solutions that meet the criteria to decide their practicality and ease of application. Identify the cost and potential results of each solution. This process will help management decide which of the possible solutions is best.

Another critical part of this phase is to name possible obstacles or barriers that may prevent applying a solution. As these barriers are named, look at them to decide the possible effects they have on various solutions. Name actions to overcome obstacles or barriers, examining financial, human, and emotional costs. This information will help you decide the best solution.

The outcome of this phase of the problem-solving process is that you will have identified the best alternative(s). Now management has an approach to follow in its quest to improve performance and enhance organizational effectiveness.

Implementation of the Solution

Internal consultants must help management carry out the best solutions(s). During this phase, the focus is on testing the solution(s) to determine its results. When doing this, choose the department, division, or unit where the solution has an opportunity for the highest degree of success. This strategy allows you to integrate the solution under the best possible conditions before you apply it to the entire organization.

Implementing solutions should be a slow and deliberate process to give you time to figure out the "real" outcomes. It is often a good idea to implement a solution in several parts of an organization before introducing it to the entire organization. Then you can refine and redesign the solution as needed.

Evaluation of the Solution

Once you have applied a solution in some proper settings, gather and compare the results. If the solution helps close the gap between expectations and performance, it can be considered a success. If, however, the gap remains the same, you may need to consider alternative solutions.

Regardless of the success or failure of a solution, the information and knowledge you gain from carrying it out is valuable. This value should be communicated to others in the organization to help them improve their understanding of the organization and the interventions that have positive and negative impacts.

Document the outcome of every intervention tried and keep an active record of the dates and location of each one. This information will be an invaluable resource for future problem-solving efforts.

FOLLOW-UP

Follow-up is the last step in the decision-making process. It is often the most overlooked and underestimated part of decision-making. But it's the step that allows you to gather accurate information about the solutions you implement and management's reaction to those solutions.

Set up follow-up procedures that ask for the perspective of managers and supervisors as well as employees, such as one-on-one personal interviews, focus groups, informal discussions, questionnaires, and reports and records.

Largely, the follow-up procedures are like those used in evaluating training programs. The primary difference is that follow-up activities show your willingness to make certain that the solutions implemented are the correct ones, since evaluation of training programs is primarily designed to gather data to support the impacts of training.

Regardless, follow-up is an excellent way to continue to enhance your credibility and image in the eyes of management and employees. You can convey your sincere interest in improving performance and organizational effectiveness, prove your talents as a professional, and continue to build deeper relationships with your clients.

INTERPERSONAL RELATIONS AND THE PROBLEM-SOLVING PROCESS

The problem-solving process allows you to have better interpersonal relationships with your clients by demonstrating communication and leadership skills and showing respect and empathy for them.

It is important for managers, supervisors, and employees to interact with each other. But it is even more important for them to communicate the meaning behind the words. The problem-solving process allows you to prove the importance of communication. You can help interpret the meaning and intent of the spoken words as well as the information shared. The result should help foster better, more trusting relationships between managers and supervisors and their employees—the first step of true communication.

The problem-solving process also allows you to differentiate between interaction and communication. Interaction is a process of exchanging information and ideas, while communication goes further into interpreting and understanding the meaning behind the information and ideas. Internal consultants have an excellent opportunity to differentiate between these two components.

Another important opportunity of this process is to demonstrate your leadership skills. In this context, *leadership* refers to initiating new ideas to overcome existing circumstances. It also includes a strength of character and a willingness to engage in complex and difficult discussions as a way to solve problems. In addition, the problem-solving process allows you to demonstrate your conviction and dedication to improving existing work conditions and to replace them with solutions and interventions that improve performance and enhance organizational effectiveness.

Another outgrowth of the problem-solving process is that it allows you to communicate respect and empathy for your clients. Respect refers to accepting clients as individuals and professionals, while empathy demonstrates your understanding of their right to have divergent opinions and methods of operation, and conflicting or competing goals and objectives.

Because the problem-solving process allows management and employees to stake out their respective positions about circumstances, situations, or events, internal consultants can show a legitimacy of both positions. You can demonstrate both respect and empathy through the interaction you have with management and employees. You can direct both parties' attention to the other's position to foster better understanding. A high level of personal integrity is needed to maintain respect and empathy for your clients and their respective positions; otherwise, you will lose credibility with them.

GROUP DYNAMICS

The problem-solving process is also an opportunity for internal consultants to demonstrate their understanding of group behavior. You can do this by using three critical characteristics of group development: (1) inclusion, (2) control, and (3) affection.

Inclusion

Internal consultants must prove their understanding of the situation to *all* group members, regardless of their status, because all group members need to feel included. Inclusion is a "sense of belonging or being a part of a greater whole."

You can demonstrate inclusion by allowing employees of less status to take part in discussions with senior management. The opinions, ideas, and recommendations of all individuals should be given equal weight. By doing this, you will clearly show your understanding and appreciation of individuals' needs to feel a part of the group.

Inclusion can also be carried out by implementing solutions and evaluating their results. Thus, individuals of lesser status are equal partners in implementing solutions and in giving information and opinions about the impact or results of solutions. This activity should, however, be a genuine effort on your part and not a contrived one designed to manipulate or coerce individuals of lesser status.

Control

The problem-solving process allows various members of the organization to take part in frank and honest discussions about the potential solutions to complex problems. Certain members of the problem-solving group are going to try to assert their authority and power over other members of the problem-solving team. While this may be proper, you must guide this process so all members of a problem-solving team have an equal opportunity to communicate their ideas and make recommendations. You should, therefore, show your respect for power and authority, while restricting individual control over the group. Then, you are modeling the positive aspects of authority and power, while decreasing its controlling aspects.

Affection

Another positive outcome of the problem-solving process is that it allows individuals to develop long-lasting relationships based on trust. A result of this type of relationship is a level of ''affection'' among team members. It allows members of the problem-solving team to set aside their respective roles and show an appreciation for one another that fosters open and honest communication.

When the group has a positive relationship, the solution identification analysis and selection processes of problem-solving become a collective effort by all team members. Better positive relationships can also improve the implementation of solutions and their subsequent evaluation. The level of affection among team members can greatly enhance the problem-solving process.

CONSULTANT SKILLS AND THE DECISION-MAKING PROCESS

At times, you will see conflict between and among team members. Then, you must use all of the consulting skills you have to identify and resolve conflicts.

Reactions to Conflict

Conflict forces people to choose among available alternatives. An individual, however, may respond to conflict in a destructive manner and become aggressive, withdrawn, or defensive.

Aggression occurs when a person directly attacks another person as a way of deflecting and defusing frustration. It tends to play itself out in physical or verbal exchanges between or among members of the decision-making team. It is, perhaps, the most harmful of all destructive methods because it results in hurt feelings and unproductive activities.

Another type of disruptive approach is *withdrawal*. Because some people are less tolerant of conflicts, they tend to withdraw within themselves rather than deal directly with the conflict. In a group situation, these individuals may change the subject, make a joke, or become silent when areas of conflict are exposed. Internal consultants need to identify this condition and try to mediate it to a positive conclusion by drawing out the individual and having them express their thoughts and feelings openly. That way, you prevent the individual from isolating himself from the group.

A final disruptive approach is becoming *defensive*. When this type of behavior is present, the focus is not on solving a problem or resolving a conflict, but is on protecting one's ego and self-esteem. A defensive person may withdraw into a fantasy or dream state, discussing unrealistic possibilities and conclusions and projecting their feelings and thoughts onto others. Another type of defensive reaction is to rationalize the reasons for their behavior or the conflict that currently exists. Or they may repress their feelings by ignoring them or denying that they exist. A common type of defensive reaction is to blame others rather than to admit feelings or thoughts.

Finally, individuals may regress into childlike behaviors as a result of conflict to deflect their feelings and thoughts.

Regardless of the reaction to conflict, internal consultants have a responsibility to make team members own up to their own thoughts and feelings. You need to set up some ground rules for the group during the decision-making process.

By establishing norms of behavior, members of the decision-making team are held accountable for their behavior and must follow the rules. For example, it may serve the purposes of a group to always refer to thoughts and feelings as "I" behaviors. This reference means individuals express their thoughts and feelings as a manifestation of themselves, not as a reflection of the thoughts and feelings of others, such as, "I feel," "I think," rather than making interpretations of how other members of the decision-making team might interpret information.

Consulting Skills

During the decision-making process, you must demonstrate a full range of consulting skills, including:

- Initiating.
- Clarifying.
- Seeking information or opinions.
- Giving information or opinions.
- Evaluating.
- Coordinating.
- Consensus testing.

Initiating.   Initiating refers to starting a group along a new path by proposing tasks and goals or suggesting a plan for handling discussions. Initiating is a consulting skill you can use to break the silence at the early stages of group discussions. You can also use it to break new ground when a group is at an impasse. Initiating demonstrates your leadership skills.

Clarifying.   Clarifying is used to interpret issues and help clear up ambiguous ideas or suggestions. You ask individuals to talk about their thoughts or feelings so the group understands them better. This skill focuses attention on alternatives and issues before the group. The group is forced to discuss issues more openly and honestly, and at the same time, in more depth and breadth.

Seeking information or opinions.   This consulting skill requires you to seek the opinions of various members of the decision-making team. You may ask for facts and relevant information on the problem, identify feelings, and seek out an understanding of what the feelings mean, or ask for information, suggestions, or ideas. This activity is very straightforward, but it is valuable for gathering information during a discussion. The best technique for gathering information is open-ended questions that solicit the opinions and ideas of a variety of individuals on the decision-making team.

Giving information.   It is often the responsibility of an internal consultant to give information or opinions to the group, because you are perceived by the group as being an expert on a subject or having unique insights into the organization. This skill requires you to offer information needed by the group to foster and improve decision-making. You must be willing to say what you believe and offer opinions, suggestions, and ideas. This skill, however, is often overused by internal consultants to enhance their credibility and confidence. It should be used at appropriate times and sparingly to provide critical data that is useful to the group.

Evaluating.   It is often important for you to evaluate ideas and suggestions to determine their practicality and realism. This skill should be used to set up a standard of judgment and provide a practical approach to evaluating outcomes and alternatives. One way you can use an evaluating skill is to teach the group to evaluate its own discussions, solutions, recommendations, and alternatives. This way, the group becomes an active participant in the evaluation process.

Coordinating.   An internal consultant should make the effort to show the relationship between ideas and recommendations, to pull together a variety of ideas and thoughts into a conceptual whole. This skill includes summarizing the discussion and recommendations of the group and offering potential decisions for the group to accept or reject. This skill may also include restating ideas, thoughts, and recommendations in a more understandable form so the group can make informed decisions.

Consensus testing. This skill is used to test whether the group is reaching a decision. It's a skill designed to set up a "trial balloon" to test the possible conclusion. This strategy is very critical because this skill is used most often to bring decision-making teams to closure. Consensus testing must be well timed and properly chosen because it can cut off critical discussion that is useful to understanding the thoughts and feelings of the decision-making team. If used inappropriately, you can alienate the group, which can severely impact your effectiveness.

GROUP THINK

One of the biggest enemies of decision-making is "group think." This is a process where the thoughts and feelings of a group reach only a certain level of understanding about a problem, its consequences, and impacts. As a result, possible alternatives, recommendations, and solutions are often not considered.

Internal consultants must guard against this shallow level of thinking. Push group members to look at all possibilities and circumstances. Become much more proactive, involved, and aggressive, and understand the importance of your role in the decision-making process.

You are not simply a member ot the group, but the leader of the group. Your primary role in the decision-making process is to push the group to a point where they can identify the best possible solution to the problem. Then, you have set up an environment for improved performance and organizational effectiveness.

VALUES OF INTERNAL CONSULTANTS

To be successful, you must have a set of values that guide your day-to-day activities. Each of the following is a value that can help you improve your efforts:

1. Credibility as a focus.
2. Responsiveness as an attitude.
3. Competence as a standard.
4. Value-added as a method of operation.
5. Professionalism as a goal.
6. Performance improvement as a given.
7. Organizational effectiveness as a way of life.
8. Quality as a standard.
9. Communication as the key to success.
10. Involvement as an ongoing effort.

Credibility

To be successful, you must establish and maintain credibility. All your efforts should reinforce credibility with managers, supervisors, and employees.

Responsiveness

Responsiveness refers to your willingness to respond to the needs and concerns of clients. Your efforts should be delivered promptly and efficiently; however, every need or concern need not be responded to equally. Responsiveness requires judgment, but the willingness to respond must always be apparent.

Competence

Internal consultants must be competent at all times. This competency includes your skills and abilities as a consultant and your knowledge of the organization and relative subject matter. Maintaining competence must be one of your performance standards. It is impossible to ask management and employees to set up performance standards if you don't have them. Therefore, it is essential that you identify the competence and performance standards that you are willing to be judged by within the organization.

Value-Added

Value-added as a method of operation means you must always make a difference. Every effort, activity, and project you engage in must be done to improve the performance and enhance the organizational effectiveness of individuals and groups. Your efforts can then easily be observed and identified by organizational decision-makers and senior management as being positive. The kiss of death for internal consultants is for management to question the value of your efforts.

Professionalism

Another driving force for internal consultants is to always maintain the highest level of professionalism. Every activity you participate in is being judged by members of the organization, including discussions, interviews, focus groups, questionnaires, training and interventions, and the decision-making process. Therefore, it is essential that you maintain the highest level of professional conduct at all times.

Performance Improvement

Performance improvement is a way of life for internal consultants. This statement summarizes the reason for your position. In Chapter 1, we differentiated between an HRD practitioner and an internal consultant. An HRD practitioner *indirectly* impacts performance improvement of individuals, while internal consultants *directly* impact this outcome. Internal consultants must constantly be focused on improving the performance of every executive, manager, supervisor, and employee in the organization. There is no greater effort you can engage in than improving performance.

Organizational Effectiveness

You directly impact the effectiveness of the organization by improving the performance of individuals. If you focus on the micro level (performance improvement), then the macro (organizational effectiveness) will result. Internal consultants should be in a constant quest of improving the working procedures, activities, and efforts of the organization, trying to continuously renew the organization and supply better ways of enhancing outcomes.

Quality

Quality is "job one" for internal consultants. Finding new and better ways to do a job, use a skill, enhance an operation, improve production, communicate, and think are all elements of quality improvement. You must focus your efforts on improving quality if individuals and organizations are going to improve. There is no value more essential to the positive outcomes of your efforts than continuous quality improvement.

Communication

One important vehicle of success for internal consultants is communication. You rely on this skill daily. In your role, you prove to the organization the power and importance of effective communication. Then, they will see the value of it too.

Involvement

To be successful, you must constantly be involved with employees and management of the organization. You must be proactive about this, always searching for ways to improve performance and enhance organizational effectiveness. Encourage change when change is proper and discourage change when it is improper. Organizational leaders should never have to ask the question, "What are our internal consultants doing?"

The decision-making process allows internal consultants to foster change. It is a systematic approach to identifying expectations and comparing them with actual performance. The result is that you define the problem—the difference between "what is and what should be"—and solve it by closing that gap.

Figure 10–1 illustrates the problem-solving process.

FIGURE 10–1
Problem-Solving Process

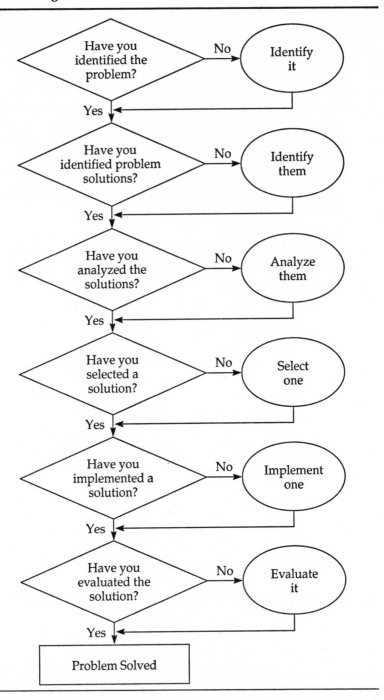

Notes

Chapter 2

1. A. N. Turner, "Consulting Is More Than Giving Advice," *Harvard Business Review* 61(5), 1983, pp. 120–29.
2. G. Lippitt and R. Lippett, *The Consulting Process*, 2nd ed. (San Diego: University Associates, 1986), p. 79.
3. A. N. Turner, "Consulting Is More Than Giving Advice," pp. 120–29.
4. C. Argyris, *Teaching Smart People How to Learn*. 1991.
5. R. Brinkerhoff, Personal Interview, 1992.
6. A. N. Turner, "Consulting Is More Than Giving Advice," pp. 120–29.
7. G. Lippitt and R. Lippett, *The Consulting Process*.
8. Ibid.
9. E. H. Neilsen, *Becoming an O.D. Practitioner* (Englewood Cliffs, N.J.: Prentice Hall, 1984), p. 17.
10. D. G. Robinson and T. C. Robinson, *Training for Impact: How to Link Training to Business Needs and Measure the Results* (San Francisco: Jossey-Bass, 1989), p. 36.
11. J. W. Gilley and S. A. Eggland, *Principals of Human Resource Development* (Reading, Mass.: Addison-Wesley Publishing, 1989), p. 176.

Chapter 3

1. G. E. Mills, R. W. Pace, and B. D. Peterson, *Analysis in Human Resource Training and Organization Development* (Reading, Mass.: Addison-Wesley Publishing, 1992).
2. J. W. Gilley, *How to Collect Data* (Alexandria, Va.: ASTD Press (InfoLine), 1990), p. 3.
3. D. G. Bowers and J. L. Franklin, *Survey-Guided Develop-*

ment I: Data Based Organizational Change (San Diego: University Associates, 1977), p. 66.

4. **G. Lippitt and R. Lippitt,** *The Consulting Process,* 2nd ed. (San Diego: University Associates, 1986), p. 82.

5. **J. W. Gilley and S. A. Eggland,** *Principles of Human Resource Development* (Reading, Mass.: Addison-Wesley Publishing, 1989), p. 205.

6. **R. Zemke and T. Kramlinger,** *Figuring Things Out: Trainers Guide to Needs and Task Analysis* (Reading, Mass.: Addison-Wesley Publishing, 1990), p. 124.

Chapter 4

1. **J. W. Gilley and S. A. Eggland,** *Principles of Human Resource Development* (Reading, Mass.: Addison-Wesley Publishing, 1989), p. 214.

2. Ibid.

3. **A. C. Daniels,** *Performance Management: Improving Quality Productivity Through Positive Reinforcement.* 3rd ed. (Tucker, Ga.: Performance Management Production, 1989), p. 56.

4. Ibid.

5. Ibid., p. 72.

6. **W. Glasser,** *Reality Therapy* (New York: Harper & Row, 1965), p. 36.

7. **A. C. Daniels,** *Performance Management.*

8. Ibid., p. 84.

9. **B. Bricker,** *Basics of Performance Technology* (Alexandria, Va.: ASTD Press (InfoLine), 1992), p. 3.

10. **A. C. Daniels,** *Performance Management,* p. 93.

Chapter 5

1. **M. L. Broad and J. W. Newstrom,** *Transfer of Training: Action-Packed Strategic to Ensure High Payoff from Training Investments* (Reading, Mass.: Addison-Wesley Publishing, 1992), p. 79.

2. Ibid., p. 98.

3. **M. S. Knowles,** "Organizations as Learning Systems," *Training and Development Journal* 40(1); pp. 5–8.

4. **Broad and Newstrom,** *Transfer of Training,* p. 122.

Chapter 6

1. **J. W. Gilley and S. A. Eggland,** *Marketing HRD Within Organizations: Enhancing the Visibility, Effectiveness, and Credibility of Programs* (San Francisco: Jossey-Bass, 1992), p. 74.

2. **R. O. Simerly,** *Strategic Planning and Leadership in Continuing Education* (San Francisco: Jossey-Bass, 1987), p. 32.

3. **L. J. Olivetti.** (Ed.) ASTD Trainer's Tool Kit: Mission Statements for HRD. Alexandria, Va.: ASTD, 1990.

4. **P. Kotler,** *Marketing Management: Analysis, Planning, and Control* (Englewood Cliffs, N.J.: Prentice-Hall, 1987), p. 32.

5. **J. W. Gilley and S. A. Eggland,** *Principles of Human Resource Development* (Reading, Mass.: Addison-Wesley Publishing, 1989), p. 245.

6. **R. O. Simerly,** *Strategic Planning and Leadership,* p. 209.

7. Ibid., p. 239.

Chapter 7

1. **J. W. Gilley and S. A. Eggland,** *Marketing HRD Within Organizations: Enhancing the Visibility, Effectiveness and Credibility of Programs* (San Francisco: Jossey-Bass, 1992), p. 2.

2. **J. W. Gilley,** "Marketing Your Human Resources Department to Your Company," *Employment Relations Today* (Summer 1992), pp. 127–32.

3. **Gilley and Eggland,** *Marketing HRD Within Organizations,* p. 28.

4. **E. M. Rogers,** *Diffusion of Innovations,* 3rd ed. (New York: Free Press, 1983, originally published 1962), p. 51.

5. **P. Kotler,** *Marketing Management: Analysis, Planning and Control,* 2nd ed. (Englewood Cliffs, N.J.: Prentice Hall, 1987), p. 129.

6. **E. J. McCarthy and W. D. Perreault,** *Basic Marketing: A Managerial Approach* (Homewood, Ill.: Irwin, 1984), p. 6.

7. **J. E. Swan and L. J. Combs,** "Product Performance and Consumer Satisfaction: A New Concept," *Journal of Marketing Research* (April 1976), pp. 25–33.

8. **Gilley and Eggland,** *Marketing HRD Within Organizations,* p. 99.

9. Ibid., pp. 130–32.

10. Ibid., p. 138.

Chapter 8

1. **D. Bienkowski,** "Ten Courses of Project Busts," *Computerworld* 5(2), 1989, p. 99.

2. **J. W. Weiss and R. K. Wysocki,** *Five Phase Project Management: A Practical Planning and Implementation Guide* (Reading, Mass.: Addison-Wesley Publishing, 1992), p. 32.

3. **A. Randolph and B. Posner,** *Effective Project Planning and Management, Getting the Job Done* (Englewood Cliffs, N.J.: Prentice Hall, 1992), p. 141.

4. **Weiss and Wysocki,** *Five Phase Project Management.*

5. **Brinkerhoff,** *Achieving Results through Training: How to Evaluate HRD to Strengthen Programs and Increase Input* (San Francisco: Jossey-Bass, 1987), pp. 63–79.

6. **Weiss and Wysocki,** *Five Phase Project Management.*

7. **E. Raudsepp,** *Handbook for Creative Managers* (New York: McGraw-Hill, 1987).

8. **G. M. Parker,** *Team Players and Teamwork: The New Competitive Business Strategy* (San Francisco: Jossey-Bass, 1990).

Index